BEYOND THE
BODYGUARD

BEYOND THE BODYGUARD

PROVEN TACTICS AND DYNAMIC STRATEGIES FOR PROTECTIVE PRACTICES SUCCESS

Gavriel Schneider

Universal-Publishers
Boca Raton

Beyond the Bodyguard:
Proven Tactics and Dynamic Strategies for
Protective Practices Success

Universal-Publishers
Boca Raton, Florida
USA • 2009

ISBN-10: 1-59942-932-2 / ISBN-13: 978-1-59942-932-8 (paperback)
ISBN-10: 1-59942-931-4 / ISBN-13: 978-1-59942-931-1 (ebook)

www.universal-publishers.com

Library of Congress Cataloging-in-Publication Data

Schneider, Gavriel.
Beyond the bodyguard : proven tactics and dynamic strategies for protective practices
success / by Gavriel Schneider.
     p. cm.
Includes bibliographical references.
ISBN-13: 978-1-59942-932-8 (pbk. : alk. paper)
ISBN-10: 1-59942-932-2 (pbk. : alk. paper)
1. Bodyguards. 2. Private security services. I. Title.
HV8290.S36 2009
363.28'9--dc22
                                                    2009010259

Cover design by Shereen Siddiqui

Photos in this book are either from the author's personal collection or
from the Dynamic Alternatives photo archives and have been used
with permission from Dynamic Alternatives (Pty) Ltd.

This book is dedicated to all those professionals
who put their lives on the line to secure others.

TABLE OF CONTENTS

Chapter 4: How to Select the Right Trainer and the Best Training Program For You

Chapter 5: Perceptions about Close Protection

Chapter 6: Terrorism, the International Environment, and Close Protection

Chapter 7: Technology, Communication, and Close Protection

Chapter 8: Use of Force Options and Close Protection

Chapter 9: Forward Thinking, Adaptability, and the Need for a Proactive Approach to Close Protection

Chapter 10: Recommendations on Standards for Close Protection Training

LIST OF ABBREVIATIONS

Abbreviation	Description
ABET	Adult-Based Education and Training
AO	Active Opposition
AOP	Attack on Principal
BG	Bodyguard
CAT	Counter Action Team
CBM	Centre Body Mass
CPO	Close Protection Operative/Officer
CQB	Close Quarters Battle
CT	Counter Terrorism
DT	Defensive Tactics
IED	Improvised Explosive Device
IAD	Immediate Action Drill
PES	Personal Escort Section
RST	Residential Security Team
RTO	Registered Training Organization
SAP	Secure Advance Party
SAS	Special Air Service
SIA	Security Industry Authority
SME	Subject Matter Expert
SOB	Security Officers Board
VIP	Very Important Person

NOTE:

The term "Close Protection" has been written in capital letters when it is used to describe the specific specialist field of security (one core concept). When describing a related aspect such as close protection team or close protection training, capital letters have not been used. The same would apply for the term "Principal" which is used to distinguish a core object and related aspects such as principal profiling which has no capital letters.

ACKNOWLEDGEMENTS

I would like to thank my fellow Directors of Dynamic Alternatives. Thanks for the support of this project: to Allen Berkowitz, Robert Schneider, and Nicole Sofianos for their assistance in editing the academic text; to my parents, family, and friends for their encouragement and support; to all my instructors, who have shared their knowledge with me; to all the professionals that I have been fortunate enough to work with over the years; to all the interview respondents for sharing their hard earned knowledge and experience; to my research supervisor Professor Anthony Minnaar for all his guidance; and, lastly, to all those persons who have not been mentioned but who have contributed to the success of this project.

PREFACE

Much of the material used to compile this book was taken from a three-year Master's Degree study on "How to professionalize the Close Protection industry in South Africa". Over 20 in-depth interviews with industry specialists including military, police, and private sector close protection operatives were conducted. In addition a full review of existing literature and practices in other countries was performed. This was coupled with my personal experience and lessons learned in over a decade of operations and training. I in no way claim that the guidelines in this book are "the only way to do things" but they have been well researched and in many cases have saved lives. I would urge anyone who truly wants to be professional to "never stop learning" and constantly strive to improve himself or herself both physically and mentally. This book is based on extensive research that was aimed at determining the current operational **skills requirements** for close protection operatives (CPOs). Operational skills refer to those skills that are vital in order for a CPO to effectively protect a designated person (this person is referred to as the "Principal").

During the research, it was found that the **task of providing Close Protection** could be divided into **various subcategories.** This was necessary in order to gain a rounded perspective of a **CPO's roles** and **duties.** CPO tasks in their entirety had to be unpacked **into their smaller subcomponents.** In fact there were many ways to subdivide the skills, requirements, and functions of CPOs. It was found that the actual subdivisions were less important than the **gaining of a comprehensive understanding of how all the aspects are interrelated and should function synergistically.**

Some key points you will learn are as follows:

This book will discuss various training related factors that were identified and examined in order to assess whether the way CPOs are trained is effective. Aspects such as the intensity, focus, duration, and content were examined. In general, it was found that it is important for the following to be implemented:

1. Effective screening and pre-training evaluation of potential trainees.

2. Training should be job orientated and focus on training CPOs for the functions that they will actually have to perform.

3. Training methodologies should focus on an outcomes based approach and utilize the fundamentals of adult based education.

4. Training should simulate reality including the related stress factors that are placed on operational CPOs such as lack of sleep and high levels of activity interspersed with boring waiting periods.

5. Ongoing training and re-training are vital components to a CPO maintaining operational competency.

6. Close protection instructors need to have both an operational background and training in instructional methodologies before being considered competent.

It is important that in the long term, international recognition of worldwide close protection qualifications is achieved. Globalization and improvements in technology have made it easier for international networking to take place. This has meant that clients are using CPOs in different countries and international comparisons are inevitable. For if CPOs are to be considered "world class," then internationally recognized minimum standards need to be implemented in the global close protection industry.

This book will also explain various trends that have a direct affect on the close protection industry, some of these include;

- Increased public awareness of international terrorism has resulted from acts such as the 9/11 attacks. This has made people more aware of the need for and benefits of security. Use of well-trained CPOs is one of the ways that potential clients are able to minimize their exposure to any potential terrorist attack.

- A CPO's ability to communicate and liaise with all relevant parties involved in the close protection environment is vital to the success of any operation. Therefore, it is essential that these aspects receive the relevant focus during training.

- A CPO needs to be well trained in use of unarmed combat and alternative weaponry. He/she can no longer rely on the use of a firearm as the primary force option.

- A CPO needs to be able to adapt to many different situations. It is important that a CPO is trained to blend in and use the correct protocol in any given situation. The focus of operations should primarily be on operating in a low-profile manner to avoid unnecessary attention.

- A CPO needs to be well trained in all aspects of planning and avoidance. The skills needed to proactively identify and avoid threats are vital to modern-day operations. The CPO also needs to be quick thinking and adaptable in order to function effectively.

+ A CPO needs to have a working knowledge of all security related aspects that could enhance the safety of his/her Principal (i.e., multi-skilled).

In addition to the above-mentioned factors, other recommendations emanating from the research that will be discussed in this book focus on minimum competency standards for the identified subdivisions of close protection. Examples of possible assessment guidelines and criteria will be identified and cover the following broad classifications:

+ prior educational qualifications
+ physical abilities
+ CPO skills
+ prior experience in guarding
+ firearm skills
+ unarmed combat
+ protective skills
+ first aid skills
+ security knowledge
+ advanced driver training
+ protocol and etiquette
+ management and business skills
+ related skills

Key Points

1. Do I want to be able to perform the duties of a CPO?
2. Am I the right person for the job?
3. Training must be job related
4. Training should be outcomes based

INTRODUCTION

Based on Startling Reality. Below is a fictional, summarized example of a busy day for a well-trained close protection professional operating in a high-risk environment.

OPERATIONAL LOGBOOK DAY 1
TIME: ZULU ALPHA 06:00

Tasking: escort of VIP Political Leader
Location: through quiet suburb

Note: full advance reconnaissance done, with identified threat of close range firearm attack

Team Leader: Team came under fire radio transcripts as follows:

"*We are under fire, we are under fire, they have come out from behind the houses. We are evacuating back to blue 1—copy roger—copy*"

"*There are four of them, using only handguns—erratic fire*"

"*Principal in hard vehicle (armored car). Principle is safe. We are evacuating to safe zone 1. Copy—roger—copy—over*"

Debrief: 07:00:   Location back at control room.

Principal is safe and taking the attack surprisingly well, considering what he has been through. He is relieved, our team acted professionally without hesitation. He is glad he employed our team.

LOGBOOK DAY 1
TIME: ZULU ALPHA 08:00

Briefing Session
Task: Advanced Hijack Avoidance Training for land and air operations

Training to be given tomorrow, to an African Royalty Protection team. Update necessary due to a kidnap threat. After training and evaluation, Alpha Team will be joining the Royal Protection Team to offer primary support. Planning team to compile advance reports—and develop primary and contingency plans.

Threat level 1 – A1/High Risk.

LOGBOOK DAY 1
TIME: ZULU ALPHA 09:00

Tasking: Meet and Greet Celebrity Beauty Queen flying in from USA on behalf of International Health Federation for AIDS Awareness. Introduce her to Bravo team leader.

ETA: 10:30   Check travel agenda and itinerary ready

Check alternative routes

Check hotel

Check restaurants

Bravo Team to escort Principal from then on.

LOGBOOK DAY 1
TIME: ZULU ALPHA 12:00 to 18:00

Tasking: Oversee Static Protection of 3 Principals from International Bank at Airport Hotel Convention Centre—High Risk—Confirmed threats

Intelligence reflects one of the Principals has had numerous death threats. The other two are High Kidnap Risks.

Coordinate venue search: Explosive dogs pick up a small explosive device found on podium. Police bomb squad called, Venue evacuated and changed to secondary location, Threat is still high but as the location of the secondary venue has been kept confidential the meeting will proceed.

LOGBOOK DAY 1
TIME: ZULU ALPHA 19:00

Phone call request to stand in on operation as manpower is short.

Tasking and Principal: Deploy as part of escort detail for West African presidential candidate visiting the country
Location Address: Country embassy
Threat Level: **Alpha 1**/High Risk – Team deployed in conjunction
                   with police units
Intelligence Reports:
                   Attempted assassination possible
Prevention Methodology:
                   Outer perimeter access control, with various cordons and
                   checkpoints including metal detectors and screening of all guests.
                   Podium and surrounding area have been swept using dogs for
                   explosive detection.
Incident report: I was positioned on the podium, scanning the crowd and confident
                   that all precautions were taken.
                   I was fatigued from earlier taskings, While scanning the crowd—I
                   saw a knife blade come out from one of the people in the crowd,
                   approximately 15 feet away. The CPO deployed in front of me took
                   the attacker down. Simultaneously the rest of the team kicked into
                   action providing cover and evacuating the Principal.
    "What would the consequences be if the presidential candidate was assassinated on foreign soil—DISASTER—which is precisely what we are preventing".

This is what can happen in the life of a top level professional CPO—and even more. *Beyond the Bodyguard* read on!

CHAPTER 1

BACKGROUND TO
THIS UNIQUE BOOK

"Absorb what is useful. Reject what is useless.
Add specifically what is your own."
—Bruce Lee

Introduction

The area of specialist/private security is a relatively under-researched field when compared to other fields. This is even more apparent when considering specialist subdivisions such as Close Protection, sometimes referred to as VIP protection or protection of designated persons. Close Protection is a holistic approach to the protection of designated individuals. It encompasses all the necessary subsectors of security knowledge and physical skills needed to ensure the protection of a person from both identified and unidentified threats as well as risks to life and personal safety.

The person receiving protection is referred to as the "Principal." In cases where the Principal is also the person financing the security operation or protection services, he/she would also be referred to as the client. It is almost impossible to keep a Principal in a 100 percent risk-free state at all times. Therefore, the primary task of a Close Protection Operative (CPO) would be to minimize the exposure of a Principal to any identified risks. The CPO's tasks must also include effective planning, which must take into account what should be done in the case of unexpected situations occurring or attacks being initiated.

The CPO therefore functions in a continuous state of identifying and assessing all relevant risks and threats, while simultaneously taking the necessary preventative measures to thwart or avoid such situations.

The CPO not only needs to be able to perform all necessary functions relating to threat assessment and risk analysis, but also, if necessary, physically implement the appropriate counter measure within

1

the constraints of the law. This would include physical combat, utilizing whatever means[1] available to neutralize attackers and maintain the safety of the Principal.

International Influences: An Overview

It is important in this modern day and age that no research topic be analyzed in isolation, especially when the topic involves the protection of peoples' lives. Globalization and the need for international benchmarking mean that it is vital for international trends to form part of this research. It is difficult to generalize about international standards and operational procedures as they vary substantially from country to country. Several international representatives from Israel, Britain, and Australia were interviewed While writing this book. Correspondence also took place with the Home Office in the United Kingdom (UK), the National Institute for Criminal Justice Research of the Department of Justice in the United States of America (USA) and the Australian Institute for Criminology.

A great deal of information was also obtained through extensive in-depth interviews with subject matter specialists. The majority of the interviewees have worked internationally and had extensive interaction with international trainers and operatives.

An Urgent Need Exists!

A need exists to clarify many aspects of the close protection industry since there is a general lack of understanding and information regarding what close protection work entails and who the kind of client that actually utilizes such a service is, let alone being able to assess what the necessary specialized training standards for CPOs should entail. Many people have a set stereotype about who and what a close protector should be. However, these stereotypes are most often incorrect or flawed, colored by public perceptions of security guards in general or news reports in the media[2].

Aims of This Book

This book addresses the problems that lie in the difficulty of an accurate analysis of the skills, training, and qualification level of CPOs that are actually operating in the world today. This book will therefore focus on the necessary operational skill requirements needed to provide effective close protection on a global scale.

---

[1]   Use of firearms, alternative weaponry or unarmed combat.

[2]   There have been reports about nightclub bouncers who are sometimes confused with CPOs.

Aspects such as candidate selection, training, and evaluation will be examined in depth. The direct question that this book aims to answer can be stated as:

> *What are the necessary operational skills requirements of and training standards for close protection officers operating in the global market?*

Key Theoretical Concepts

For the purposes of this book, the following key definitions will apply. The industry jargon defined below is vital for the reader to understand the book. (Additional terms are defined in Appendix: Definitions):

Bodyguard: The person on a close protection team directly responsible for the Principal and closest to the Principal at all times. People often confuse bodyguards with all CPOs. The bodyguard is one of the roles a CPO may assume.

Client: The person, body or organization that is financing the close protection operation.

Close Protection: The carrying out of all necessary activities by a team or individual to ensure the safety, comfort, and peace of mind of a Principal.

Close Protection Operative/Officer: Either an individual or member of a close protection team that facilitates close protection.

Close Protection Team: A group of well-trained CPOs that operate in a synergistic manner, fulfilling all the tasks necessary to ensure the safety, comfort, and peace of mind of a Principal/Principals.

International community: Within the context of this book, this term refers to the organizations, groups, and individuals that are actively involved in the facilitation, training or any other related activity of close protection. i.e., that carry out their respective operations internationally.

Operational skills: Those skills that a CPO must posses in order to provide effective close protection to a designated Principal.

Principal: The individual receiving close protection services.

Risk analysis: The process of assessing the likelihood of threats occurring, based on aspects such as the environment, the Principal, and his or her scheduled movements.

Security: All the applicable measures needed to ensure the safety of a country, company or individual against espionage, theft or other danger/threat.

Threat assessment: The procedure undertaken to identify, categorize, validate and plan for any threats that the Principal may be exposed to.

VIP: Acronym for a "Very Important Person." The term is interchangeable with that of Principal.

Summary – How This Book Can Help You If You Are Currently a CPO or Want to Be Part of This Elite Field

CPOs can provide a more professional and improved close protection service and therefore enhance their capability to keep themselves and their Principal secure and safe (protected from all possible threats).

CPO trainers and instructors stand to benefit since they will have a reference to training material and standards in order to compare their current practices and training methods or standards. In addition, the material will provide them with an opportunity to be exposed to identified trends and changes, particularly from the international scene. This will enable them to adapt their training programs and methodologies to ensure that at least a minimum standard is met by all trainees found competent.

Security as a whole is a much-neglected field of research, when compared to many other industries. Therefore, the specialist area of close protection is an area that has almost completely been ignored with regard to formal research. There have also been many technological developments, global changes, and other changes that may not be have been included or may have been overlooked in current close protection training methodologies.

Local and international trends have seen a large-scale growth in the close protection industry and private security industry in general. There are several relevant factors that have contributed to this trend, which have in turn led to a need for the regulation of a growing industry.

Accordingly, this book will assist and benefit not only the regulatory bodies in achieving fair and valid standards and practices but also individual CPOs, as well as close protection trainers.

CHAPTER 2

A VIEW INSIDE THE CLOSE PROTECTION INDUSTRY

"The expectations of life depend upon diligence;
the mechanic that would perfect his work,
must first sharpen his tools"
—Confucius

Historical Development of Close Protection

Close Protection is as old as mankind and warfare. Quotes referring to persons fulfilling close protection roles can even be traced back to the Bible. A clear example of this is the reference to King Solomon's bodyguards protecting him while he sleeps:

"Behold his bed, which is Solomon's; threescore valiant men are about it, of valiant Israel. They all hold swords, being expert in war; every man has his sword upon his thigh because of fear in the night" (Song of Solomon, verses 7 and 8, Chapter 3).

Fairly comprehensive historical summaries can be found in several other publications on the subject. In essence, as soon as the proliferation of survival instincts came to the fore of people's behavior, it was inevitable that the stronger members of primitive clans would protect the weaker members from any outside threats or attacks.

Some of the earliest written records of protectors refer to the ancient Roman Praetorian Guards who were responsible for the protection of the ruling emperor.

It is fair to say that as soon as rulers of almost any race in any region came into power, there were probably a select few chosen to protect these rulers (the operative term being "with their lives"). These "protectors" were probably chosen for their physical strength and martial skills, which obviously favored the weapons of that day—for example, the use of the sword by Samurai in ancient Japan.

Many key principles of Close Protection can even be traced back to the ancient text known as *The Art of War* which was written over 2,000 years ago by the Chinese military strategist Sun Tzu.

Key Principles

1. Proactive planning
2. Avoidance
3. Know yourself
4. Know your enemy

Among the many applicable concepts and tactics, which are as relevant today as they were when the Sun Tzu's book was written, is the idea of **proactive planning** and **avoidance** to achieve objectives.

On this point, Sun Tzu stated the following:

> "*Know the enemy and know yourself; in a hundred battles
> you will never be defeated. When you
> are ignorant of the enemy but know yourself,
> your chances of winning or losing are equal.
> If ignorant of both your enemy and yourself,
> you are sure to be defeated in every battle*"
> —Tzu, 500 B.C.: 106

The above quote can be directly translated to the well-accepted close protection adage often mentioned in close protection training material and sometimes referred to as the "Seven P's of Close Protection," namely *"Prior proper planning and preparation, prevents poor performance."* (Dynamic Alternatives: 20). In the modern-day world of specialist security, Close Protection is as accepted as any other relevant security function. However, many of the interview respondents when asked about outside perceptions of Close Protection made comments similar to the one below:

Self Test

• What did I learn?
• How, when and why will I best put it into practice and what is the best way I will do this?

> "*The overall objectives, the attributes of the operatives and
> the manner in which the job is performed
> are still for the most part misunderstood
> by those not directly involved*"
> —David M. Sharp

Several films on the subject such as *The Bodyguard* and *In the Line of Fire*' have added to the mystique of Close Protection. However, even though there are certainly aspects of Close Protection that are accurately portrayed in such films there are in fact many more questionable practices that are demonstrated in these films (e.g., in *The Bodyguard* only one CPO attempts to protect the Principal in a high-threat situation that clearly would require a close protection team). These misconceptions are understandable since the films were created purely for entertainment value and not meant in any way to be realistic portrayals of close protection operations.

There is no doubt that over the years many variables including technology and experience have led to the improvement and adaptation of protective practices. Based on personal experience and validated in almost every interview conducted during the research for this book, the realities of modern-day close protection are quite different from the purely physical function (body protection of client/Principal) that was performed by early "protectors." When describing what can be termed the "modern approach," much time is spent on advance planning, paperwork, and the like as opposed to the glorified images seen in the movies.

The realities of long hours, poor treatment and, very often, relatively low remuneration seem to be commonplace in the way that protective services are being currently provided in the world today.

Moreover, when considering the professional attitude and focused approach of modern-day close protection specialists it is difficult not to be impressed. The individuals providing protection have developed the ability to blend in to almost any environment. Although they may look like everyone else in a crowd or on a street, both in dress and mannerisms, at the same time they are capable of quick-thinking reactions and decisive or rapid decision making. Accordingly, well-trained operatives in the close protection field have the special ability to deal with a multitude of dangerous situations in different environments in a very effective manner.

Key Principles

1. Collect knowledge and use of technology and expertise
2. Advanced planning
3. Endurance of long hours
4. Professional attitude
5. Formal approach
6. Ability to blend into any environment
7. Capable of :
   - Quick of thinking–reactions, and
   - Decisive, rapid decision making

As this field developed and adjusted to meet the demands of a changing world so too have the requirements of the Principals seeking this service.

It is vital that the link between provision of service and client demands and needs be addressed.

This is required in order to make sure that CPOs are providing protection in the most effective manner for today's environmental and situational demands.

Increase in the Demand for Professional Close Protection Operatives

Self Test

List 5 groups of people that make use of close protection services

There are several aspects that need to be outlined when looking at the increase in demand for close protection operatives. Several of these are not new ideas. However, globalization and the ease of access to information through the Internet and other media sources have made the previous reasons (these will be outlined later in this section) for why Principals may have needed protection even more applicable. The rationale discussed below is not listed in any order of priority, importance or preference. It should be noted that in different regions each reason may be of greater or of lesser importance.

i) Kidnap and ransom

The first key reason for the need for protection services by individuals, families or companies to be discussed is the threat of kidnap and ransom. In general the victims of kidnap and ransom situations would be high profile and fit into one of the following group classifications:

+ political
+ celebrity
+ influential
+ wealthy
+ personal/other

It is accepted and outlined in most relevant literature that one of the most effective ways of minimizing the chances of kidnap occurring is to utilize the services of a well-trained close protection detail. This has become even more important as the earnings of most prominent public company CEOs and directors have become public knowledge (forced disclosure for reasons of transparency and good governance) and at times even being published in newspapers.

This aspect is a trend that was identified during the in-depth interview process. Several of the respondents predicted that kidnapping would increase in the future.

The reasoning behind this was that as physical security measures and prevention technologies for preventing current common crimes become more effective (for example, at private homes or company offices), criminals will seek other ways to make money. Kidnapping is an obvious, lucrative alternative, currently having less of a security threat (being caught by the police or deterred by security measures) to the perpetrators.

ii) Terrorist activities

The second key reason is the proliferation of international media coverage of terrorist activities and criminal violence. This has made people more aware than ever before of terrorist threats and has led to people, who may not have utilized CPOs in the past, now making use of their professional services.

A sentiment often mentioned by respondents in interviews was that the terrorist attacks of 11 September 2001 (9/11) have forever changed the world's view on

Recent political rally held in London.
(Note the violent nature of comments on the posters.)

security and the existing threat of potential terrorist attack. While terrorism is not new, the attacks of 9/11 demonstrated that many people who consider themselves safe were actually still vulnerable, since most (future) terrorist activities would be very difficult for anyone to forecast and therefore avoid. Effective and ongoing threat and risk analysis, which forms the backbone of any close protection operation, is probably one of the most reliable ways of minimizing exposure to potential terrorist attack.

For this reason alone many clients, who previously may have felt that employing CPOs was an unnecessary expense and inconvenience may have changed and still may change their approach, post-9/11. An example of this is how it has become policy for many large international companies to provide more stringent security for their top executives worldwide in the aftermath of the 9/11, London, and Bali bombings.

iii) Increasing levels of violent crime

The third reason is increased levels of violent crime (perceived and otherwise) and the associated feelings of insecurity and safety. The proliferation of **violent** crime and terror worldwide are definite reasons why clients may feel the need to seek close protection services. Even though crime occurs worldwide, the topic is particularly relevant in countries such as South Africa. The South African example will be used to highlight this point. A common theme that is echoed by criminals is that they target persons who seem unaware or "easy victims."

With the comparatively high levels of violent crime in South Africa, certain international companies with operations in South Africa have

Armed robbery and carjacking are common crimes in many Third World countries.

made provision for close protection services to be provided, not only for visiting, high-profile executives, but also for expatriate employees that are residing in this country for brief periods. One American company has gone as far as to allocate each expatriate family with a dedicated CPO to handle all of the security needs for the duration of its stay in the country. In addition, it is becoming a valid risk management activity for large companies to employ CPOs tasked with the safeguarding of top company executives from becoming the victims of everyday crime.

There is also the advent of international criminal syndicates (ICS), which utilize acts of terror to achieve their criminal objectives. These organizations are operating across borders in certain cases their activities could be classified mainly as criminal acts since their primary aim may be extortion for profit. They may use acts of terror as a tool to achieve intimidation of potential competition or law enforcement agencies. Therefore, in such situations all the benefits and approaches of utilizing close protection professionals that have been previously discussed would be as relevant for minimizing the risks of becoming a victim of international crime as for acts of terror.

Self Test

• What have you learned?

• How are you going to implement?

iv) The paparazzi and media phenomenon

The fourth reason given for the need and use of close protection services result from the activities of paparazzi[3] and media phenomenon. This aspect is primarily applicable to celebrities or high-profile persons.

---

[3]   Paparazzi is the term used to describe journalists and photographers that basically "stalk" celebrities in order to obtain controversial stories or take revealing or contentious photographs.

Although public interest in famous persons is nothing new, the methods of access to information (for example, easy access to information on the Internet) have made it far easier for members of the media to obtain information on persons of public interest (information could include their movements, where they are staying, what functions they are attending, etc.).

In their ongoing pursuit of information and photographs, many paparazzi in effect stalk celebrities. This results in the celebrity having almost no privacy and being constantly inconvenienced. A relatively effective countermeasure is to employ a close protection detail that, along with providing the standard personal security, will put in place the relevant physical security measures (such as access control and perimeter security) thereby enhancing the privacy of the Principal and making access for unwanted persons extremely difficult.

v) Government outsourcing
The fifth reason for the growth in demand and the use of CPOs has been an increase in government outsourcing of such services. This is an international trend, which sees close protection tasks that were originally considered the sole preserve and responsibility of state agencies (police, military, intelligence or other government organizations/institutions) being outsourced to private companies.

> **Self Test**
>
> Name 5 reasons for use of CPO

Having Your Finger on the Pulse—Overview of Current Information
The majority of literary material available on Close Protection as a subject fits into one of two broad categories. The first is autobiographical or anecdotal which generally involves operatives recounting their personal experiences while providing protective services.

The second are non-fiction books or training manuals, which focus on the instructional and relevant operational skills required to effectively provide protection to a designated person. After a comprehensive review, it was found that the autobiographical material contained very little usable information as related to the specifications of this research. As a result of this, the focus has been on instruction-based literature.

One of the primary aims of this book has been to consolidate all information available into a generic format to enable the reader to have a summarized overview of what Close Protectors do and how they are trained to do it. Basically this is in order to highlight the established operational skills requirements of CPOs, since this is one of the key focus areas outlined in this book.

Overall, with reference to the four essential outcomes, which will be outlined later in this chapter, the concept of gathering as much information as possible before planning and/or attempting to conduct an operation makes obvious sense. Many other books and manuals that were reviewed follow this format. The starting point for any protection operation is the "Principal's Brief," which would include conducting a comprehensive principal profile, collecting and assessing as much information on the Principal's itinerary and/or movements and, lastly, conducting an ongoing comprehensive threat assessment and risk analysis.

Further key areas for practical training and deployment have been identified namely: protection on foot, protection in transit and protection at venues. The necessary hard skills such as firearms and armed/unarmed combat actually needed to protect a Principal during these movements usually then fall into these subdivisions respectively.

Definition and Job Description

For the purposes of this book:

> **Close Protection can be defined as implementing
> all necessary tasks and related activities by trained
> professionals in order to primarily ensure the safety
> and security of a designated person ("Principal").
> This safety also implies the Principal's peace of mind
> and, if possible, physical comfort.**

There are many different variations in definitions of CPOs and their job descriptions. However, irrespective of the complexity, detail or even simplicity of any of these definitions, there appear to be three factors that are common throughout. All three are contained and can be discerned from the above definition, namely:

1. Ensuring the Principal's safety
2. Ensuring the Principal's peace of mind
3. Ensuring the Principal's comfort

All three are expanded upon and discussed in greater detail below:

Ensuring your Principal's safety

This is the key fundamental, which at first glance may appear straightforward and simple, but even some of the best presidential protection units in the world cannot give an absolute guarantee of safety to their leaders. It is often stated that what can be offered within reason is the best possible protection in any given situation. When referring to safety we are not only referring to the safety from physical attack but also the health of the Principal, the safety of his family, and the security of his possessions and business interests.

Ensuring your Principal's peace of mind
This refers to the protection of the Principal's integrity, public standing, and associated aspects. The CPO is a representative of his/her Principal and any actions of the CPO could have possible negative repercussions for the Principal. This could have serious implications if the media reports these actions in a negative light. Your Principal has to know that you have his or her best interests in mind and that you can be trusted.

During the course of protecting a Principal, a CPO may be exposed to classified and/or sensitive information about the Principal and his or her business interests or even family/personal life. It is vitally important that the CPO has the complete discretion and integrity to keep this information strictly to him/herself. If the Principal cannot even trust the persons assigned to protect their life, what sort of peace of mind would they have?

Ensuring your Principal's comfort
This is the third concept outlined in the job description definition, even though it is most definitely **not** the primary function of a CPO. Having said that, if it does not expose the Principal to higher risk the CPO should try to make sure that the Principal is physically comfortable. If the Principal appears to be safe then the majority of a CPO's duties will be focused on ensuring the physical comfort of the Principal.

As an example to clarify this point, certain specialists feel a CPO should never carry shopping bags for the Principal, but if it is a low-level client with very little risk and he/she would struggle to walk because of being overloaded with parcels, it would be most improper for the CPO to not assist since even if an attack took place the CPO could drop the bags and engage the threat.

*A CPO in position securing the door
before a VIP exits a private jet.*

Profile of a CPO

> *"The CPO must conduct him/herself in a manner synony-*
> *mous with the Principal at all times"*
> —David M. Sharp

By consolidating the key concepts in most of the documents that were reviewed, the following job description for a CPO was compiled:

+ The modern-day[4] close protection operative must be able to blend easily into any situation.

+ Since the modern-day protector spends a great deal of time with a client, he must carry him/herself with an air of respected and respectful professional authority, which can only be gained through realistic, thorough training and experience.

+ The modern-day close protector is a security specialist proficient in all areas related to protection. He/she must be able to operate as an individual or as part of a high-risk professional protection team.

+ A close protection operative must be as functional on the shooting range, as at diplomatic functions or dinner parties. When a protector is assigned to a high-level client, he/she not only assumes the risks of that client but also becomes a representative of the client.

Self Test

- What have I learned?
- How, when, why am I best going to implement it?

This means that all the actions of the protector are considered a direct reflection on the client. Therefore, the actions, behavior, and public relations skills of the modern-day protector must be in line with those of his client, in order to perform effectively in the modern-day protective environment.

Essential Training Outcomes Needed to Operate as a Professional CPO

Essential outcome 1: Determine the Principal's brief and risk profile in all environments and circumstances.

Essential outcome 2: Plan the transit/foot/venue protection operation of a Principal.

Essential outcome 3: Protect a Principal during transit/foot/venue movements and static situations.

Essential outcome 4: Terminate and review protection operation.

---

[4] The stereotype of a large aggressive individual wearing a suit and dark sunglasses and brandishing a firearm is far removed from the modern-day professionals who are trained to provide a comprehensive service in this highly specialized industry.

(These outcomes were originally taken and modified from the South African Qualification Authorities' (SAQA) Unit Standard 11510: Provide protection of designated persons. This unit standard has now expired and been replaced with a more detailed qualification.)

Essential outcome 1: Determine the Principal's brief and risk profile in all environments and circumstances.

The concept of gathering as much information as possible before planning and/or attempting to conduct an operation makes obvious sense. The "Principal's Brief"[5] would include conducting and formulating a comprehensive "principal profile,"[6] assessing and collecting as much information on the Principal's itinerary or movements, and, lastly, conducting a comprehensive threat assessment and risk analysis. Such analysis to include aspects of the Principal's business and political interests, business and political contacts, or any other relevant information or external factors that could have an impact on the levels of risk associated with the persona of the Principal.

This takes into account who would threaten a Principal, why would he be threatened, what form would the threat take and how would it be implemented—e.g., if your Principal is a high-profile political figure visiting a foreign country, what are the possibilities of an assassination attempt by a sniper and how would you counteract this?

Essential outcome 2: Plan the transit/foot/venue protection operation of a Principal.

Once the threats, risks, and movements of the Principal have been determined, comprehensively plan what needs to take place. In order to provide comprehensive protection, planning needs to encompass the three aspects outlined above, namely protecting the Principal while at **venues**, in **transit** or moving on **foot**. The Principal needs to be protected wherever he/she goes. Therefore arrangements must be made in order to be able to protect the Principal while in transit (flying,

Key Principles

1. Determine Principal's Brief and risk profile
2. Plan protection operation
3. Protect Principal at all stages
4. Terminate protection operation

---

[5] The Principal's Brief explains the way in which the Principal would like the protection detail to be run and his/her specific preferences.

[6] The principal profile is an ongoing process of gathering all useful information regarding all relevant aspects related to the Principal such as lifestyle, personality, history, personal relationships, etc. These would be formatted into a document that would outline all the applicable information.

driving, etc.), while moving on foot and, lastly, at any venues or places where the Principal may be staying or visiting.

This requires that you plan for all worst-case scenarios and all realistic threat and risk scenarios.

A more practical example is that it does not matter whether the Principal is attacked in his/her hotel room or his/her house since the bottom line is that planning should have identified the likelihood of either occurrences and the necessary avoidance or counter measures, i.e., contingency plans put in place. Even if this was not done, the CPOs should have been sufficiently trained to effectively manage (spontaneously respond as their training has taught them to) the attack and counter attack, and defend and keep the Principal alive.

Essential outcome 3: Protect a Principal during transit/foot/venue movements and static situations.

Once comprehensive planning has been conducted, make resources available and allocate the actual protection for the operation to be conducted. A key idea that is applicable at this stage is the implementation of a flexible and adaptable approach. For performance of protection operations, you need to have extensive back-up and contingency plans available and work them out in advance. It is assumed that the persons being utilized to provide the protection are all trained professionals and competent in all the sub-areas of protection (the latter will be described in the second part of this book.)

> **Self Test**
> ---
> • Name the general environments in which a Principal must be protected
> • What must you have in advance?
> • What happens at termination of operation?

Essential outcome 4: Terminate and review protection operation.

After the operation is completed, it is necessary to conduct a debriefing in order to learn from any mistakes that may have occurred and to receive feedback from all parties involved. All relevant documentation needs to be collected and consolidated in case it will be used for another operation, as well as to maintain operational security. At this stage, CPOs normally submit task reports to be utilized by the team leader who will normally compile a full Operational Review report.

CHAPTER 3

UNDERSTANDING WHAT MAKES A CPO

"Courage, above all things,
is the first quality of a warrior"
— Karl Von Clausewitz

In order to effectively summarize and group the relevant information into a workable format, a generic categorization has been used, which presents the relevant material in a logical manner. It is important to note that subject matter breakdown (into the categories below) will be further broken down into additional subdivisions. These categories are not listed in order of priority or importance.

Subject Matter Breakdown
1. Protective skills
2. Unarmed combat and close quarter battle (CQB) skills
3. Firearm and relevant tactical skills
4. First aid and relevant medical skills
5. Security
6. Driver training
7. Protocol and etiquette
8. Written fieldwork
9. Related skills

These individual yet interrelated topics will be explained in the following section. This subject matter breakdown refers to the aspects of Close Protection that are standard within the majority of texts that were examined. In the various publications and manuals there are often differences in technical jargon but once analyzed it became clear that the operational principles, outline, and job descriptions are generally consistent. (The above-mentioned subdivisions will be outlined below.)

CPO Protection Skills

This field comprises the following subjects:

Applied protection: The two formations – individual and group

This provides an overview of how protective teams are manned, the general roles and duties, as well as certain concepts as applied to team dynamics. The aim of the material dealing with this subject is to provide an overview of team and operational structure. Moreover, it is impossible to understand the structure of a protection detail fully unless the key roles and duties of Close Protection are better understood.

CPOs in a diamond formation functioning as the Personal Escort Section (author is at the front of the formation).

The Personal Escort Section (PES)

Often referred to as the moving shield around a Principal, these are the members of the close protection team that move with the Principal. CPOs operating in this role attempt to fulfill six primary functions and tasks, namely:

+ To **protect** the Principal by shielding him/her physically with the CPO's body
+ To **divert** potential attack away from the Principal by being an extra target for the attacker to deal with
+ To **rescue** the Principal by removing him/her from the immediate vicinity of the incident
+ To **neutralize** an attacker by means of any methods or combat skills (only if this preserves the Principals' life and no other alternatives are available)
+ If necessary **support** the Principal's life by providing first aid until more qualified help arrives

+ To **liaise** with authorities in order to enlist their assistance in preventing or combating an incident

The Personal Escort Section (PES), as a direct result of the duties they perform, represent the Principal in the public perception more then many other of the close protection functions. This can be directly attributed to the close proximity to the Principal in which PES members operate.

The Secure Advance Party (SAP)

The role of the Secure Advance Party—also known as the *Security* Advance Party—is primarily to provide as much information as possible before a Principal undertakes any action, activity or excursion. Information to be collected by the SAP includes details on the routes, venues, logistical considerations, liaisons with applicable contact persons, situational and environmental threats, and/or any other relevant information that may concern the Principal or the PES team. The SAP may travel from location to location before the PES and the Principal arrive or once the Principal arrives merge with the PES team and then primarily operate in that role.

The Residence Security Team (RST)

The Residence Security Team's (RST) duties are primarily to secure and protect the Principal's residence. It does not matter what or where the Principal's residence is (mansion, flat, yacht or hut), the team designated to protect this is fulfilling the operational definition of a RST. Residence security itself focuses mainly on the application of physical security measures such as alarms, lighting, access control, etc. The RST are the persons who run and manage these physical measures as well as handle the relevant human factor security issues such as patrols and access control.

Venue protection

Venue protection involves all the applied security actions taken to ensure the safety of the Principal when he/she is visiting places or locations other than his/her home *or* working environment. The concept of protection at various venues focuses primarily on the positioning of manpower in different situations according to the physical layout, information collected during advance work, available manpower, the Principal's wishes and, of course, the relevant threats. Most reviewed literature provides preferred positioning of manpower in the following situations:

+ at restaurants
+ movies or theatres
+ functions and ceremonies

- rallies or events
- presentations or speaking engagements.

The protection principles taught using these examples provide a basis for understanding of how to position the protective detail in almost any situation.

Protection principles and techniques

Immediate action drills (IADs) are planned, trained responses to an attack or specified situation. In certain manuals, several IADs were explained in considerable detail but the primary examples described and explained are:

- an attack with a firearm at different ranges
- an attack with a knife
- hand grenade attack
- unarmed close quarters attack

There are slight differences in the way that IADs are performed. However, there is common ground in all of them when describing the key aspects such as awareness techniques, communications, and reactions. Almost all of these include engagement and evacuation as well as applied team tactics based on the number of team members involved.

Counter Action Teams (CAT)

Counter Action Teams (CAT) refer to teams that accompany the Principal and the PES, usually found at the rear of a motorcade or at the back of the close protection detail. The CAT team usually has received more extensive tactical training and therefore has increased capability with regards to counter attack and tactical intervention techniques. Their primary function would be to respond in the case of an attack situation.

In an attack, the CAT team would aggressively counterattack the "active opposition" (AO) while the PES and bodyguard evacuate the Principal. In extreme situations, members of the CAT team may also function as counter snipers providing cover for the close protection detail.

Unarmed combat and Close Quarter Battle (CQB)/Self Defense

It is a logical concept to understand that before an individual is capable of protecting someone else they must first have the capability to defend themselves. Certain manuals advocate a martial arts approach, but the more progressive literature focuses on the practical application of effective techniques and principles necessary to restrain, incapacitate or neutralize an attacker.

This subject can be further subdivided as follows:

Unarmed combat

Unarmed combat refers to the use of natural body weapons (e.g., hands and feet) and similar defensive strategies to effectively disengage from confrontation or disable and neutralize an attacker if necessary. Natural body weapons include any part of the body that could be utilized to inflict harm on an attacker (head, hands, elbows, feet, etc.). It also includes all relevant techniques found in combat applicable martial arts such as joint locking, throwing, and wrestling.

Certain manuals concentrate on the accessing of pressure and nerve points as an effective part of their unarmed combat strategy. This topic will be expanded on in the chapter on use of force and close protection.

Edged weapon combat

Edged weapon combat applies to the use of bladed weapons, like knives or any other implement that can be utilized in a cutting or stabbing like motion. This topic is totally absent from a fair amount of literature. This is possibly due to the complexity of its nature and the conflicting opinions on what is effective and what is not. The concept of "knife fighting" as applied to Close Protection focuses primarily on the capability to defend against edged weapon attack.

It should be noted that in order to effectively defend against a weapon, it is vital that an operative must first understand how it works.

The author demonstrating defense against an edged weapon attack. (Note the rest of the equipment on the tactical belt that would normally be concealed during a protection operation.)

Otherwise there is no way of knowing what to expect and it is impossible to defend against something when the methods of application are not known by the defender.

Improvised weapon combat

Improvised weapon combat includes the use of any environmental tool that can be utilized for self-defense in the case of an attack (e.g., pens, sticks or stones, and rocks). This becomes very important in Close Protection since when operating internationally, a CPO may not be allowed to carry any weaponry at all with him/her into another country. Therefore, the CPOs ability to deal with attack has to become more reliant on the use of weapons that can be found in the general or immediate environment. The increasing importance for CPOs to possess this capability is becoming universally accepted.

Use of alternative weapons

Alternative weapons are weaponry other than firearms and edged weapons that may be utilized by CPOs as part of their operational equipment. Examples of alternative weaponry are tools such as the ASP baton stun guns, handcuffs, mace or pepper spray.

The CPO's ability to utilize alternative weapons provides a platform from which it is easier to comply with legalities such as use of minimum force during self-defense. It also enables the CPO to better defend against such weapons should the need arise as he/she would have a working knowledge of how an attacker would effectively utilize such tools.

Restraint and control techniques

Restraint and control tactics are those techniques and practices that enable an attacker to be subdued without any permanent damage or injury being inflicted on him/her. This subfield is of more importance to strictly law enforcement personnel than to CPOs. There is, however, a trend for certain close protection details that have enough manpower to focus on utilizing these techniques. An example of this would be in applying the tactic of "swarming," where a large number of CPOs literally swarm all over the attacker(s), overwhelming him/her by sheer numbers and weight but not actually striking or inflicting injury on the attacker in the process.

Team tactics and applied unarmed combat

The concept of team tactics refers to the manner in which a close protection team would implement their unarmed combat and close quarter battle (CQB) into their IADs. Applied unarmed combat means that whatever techniques and tactics that are taught to CPOs need to be practiced and implemented into the Close Protection function as a whole.

All of these concepts become increasingly important when considering close protection operations in crowds and when multiple attackers are involved, including unarmed combat and related IADs for various contingencies.

The main example cited in most manuals was that of restraining over-zealous fans who, while not wishing to hurt the Principal, may end up doing so as they are not in control of their actions, e.g., pressure or force of crowd behind them pushing to get near a Principal.

Firearm Skills

The use of firearms in close protection situations has become a topic of considerable debate and controversy worldwide. This has huge ramifications for CPO training and operations as one should always operate within the laws of one's own country but if working internationally, firearm skills are important. **A relatively comprehensive platform for the use of firearms while performing close protection functions and related firearms guidelines is outlined below:**

Basic firearm understanding and training
The key concepts that are taught under this heading would fall primarily into one of three areas namely:
- safe handling of firearms,
- maintenance of firearms,
- basic marksmanship.

CPOs on the shooting range firing from a kneeling position.
(Note that this photo is taken from a series
that involved CPOs transitioning from standing
to kneeling and then to prone position.)

The concepts and principles taught in this subfield, form a foundation on which to build further training. Due to the nature of close protection work an armed CPO must possess a high level of competency with regards to the usage of firearms. This is vital within the context of the following aspects relevant to CPO work.

+ Crowds: CPOs often work in crowds, a situation in which inaccurate firing of a firearm or over penetration (i.e., a bullet going right through a target) could harm innocent civilians/bystanders.

+ Firing and movement: The majority of IADs utilizing firearms involve firing and movement, which is difficult to perform unless good training and constant retraining is in place.

+ Firing distances: The range (distance) at which the CPO will have to shoot often varies, meaning that a CPO has to have the necessary skills to compensate for sudden changes in range and conditions (i.e., visibility, rain, wind, trajectory, downhill/uphill, etc.).

Target shooting skills

Target shooting skills specific to Close Protection refers to the ability of a CPO or team to be able to effectively shoot and hit various targets from different positions in different places and conditions. This denotes shooting and movement, shooting from cover and vehicles, as well as implementation of IADs with firearms. The ability of a CPO to be able to fire quickly and accurately is vital.

There are different schools of thought concerning targeting. However, most professionals seem to agree that the focus of training should be to hit "centre mass" (the centre of the human body) with the additional ability to fire accurate head shots being secondary. In other words, the CPO must be able to accurately hit the centre mass with multiple shots while moving and implementing the appropriate immediate action drill(s).

Key Principles

1. Provide cover
2. Divert attack
3. Neutralize attacker
4. Evacuate Principal

Firearm close quarter battle (CQB) skills

Firearm close quarters battle (CQB) denotes the use of the firearm at extreme close ranges in conjunction with unarmed combat (this includes not only firing the weapon but also striking with it as well as utilizing unarmed combat techniques). As stated above in the subsection on "the range of engagement," the distance of an attack may vary and change very quickly. This, as well as the fact that in many situations CPOs operate in crowds, means that the capability of a CPO to effectively draw and use a firearm at close range is an important part of his/her ability to effectively deal with attack or multiple attacks and/ or attackers.

Urban movement and house penetration skills
This concept refers to utilizing the firearm in combat related situations that may occur in built up areas where the CPO may have to move through obstacles and buildings safely and quickly. The main principle focuses on how to keep oneself behind cover and move when necessary while still being able to effectively engage and neutralize the enemy.

When looking at this skill in the context of a Close Protector's role it is clearly not the same as a tactical or intervention operator whose roles may include tasks such as engaging in hostage rescue. Rather the CPO may need these skills primarily when separated from the Principal who may be under attack and the CPO must get to and evacuate a Principal in such a manner that would provide the minimum exposure to the existing threat.

Night/low-light shooting skills
The ability to fire accurately in low-light conditions as well as utilize torches or illumination devices (such as laser pointers or illuminated sights) while engaging the attacker is an important skill for close protection operatives that may have to work in varying environments at different times (i.e., in a hotel, at an office, at the Principal's residence or even

CPOs performing low-light firearms training.
(Note the front CPO is using a shotgun,
while the CPO behind is armed only with a pistol.)

25

while in transit). There has been much technological advancement in the field of low-light shooting, including red-dot sights, laser sights, and torch attachments clipping directly onto the firearm. In extreme circumstances, even night-vision scopes are available. However, these would rarely be applicable to the protection role of CPOs.

Protection team and single operative firearm skills

This subfield focuses on the use of firearms as related to Close Protection. This involves various techniques as a single operative or team integrating protective strategies and techniques. The generic aims would be to provide cover for the Principal, divert the attack away from the Principal, neutralize the attacker and then evacuate the Principal while firing or being in such a position to be able to fire. These could also include actions while driving and getting into or out of vehicles.

These drills need to be rehearsed until they are instinctive. This is vital since if a CPO or team is not well versed in such tactics and able to respond instinctively there could well be delays in providing protection to the Principal, which in itself could have disastrous outcomes. Innocent civilians, the Principal, and team members could be shot or hurt if these drills are not effectively conducted.

Firearm disarming skills

When considering the huge advantage that attackers will have over the Protection Team because of surprise, it is vital for a CPO to have the ability to disarm an attacker who is pointing a firearm at either him/her, another CPO, his/her Principal or at a crowd. This aspect goes hand-in-hand with effective unarmed combat skills. Competencies should include being able to stop a potential attacker from drawing a weapon as well as to disarm an attacker that may already have his or her firearm out.

Firearm retention skills

Retention refers to the CPO's ability to prevent an attacker from disarming him/her. The CPO needs to have the necessary skills to maintain control of his or her own firearm whether in the holster position or drawn and in use. This skill is also closely linked to the CPO having effective unarmed combat ability. As with disarming techniques, the CPO must possess techniques to retain the weapon when moving through crowded areas while the weapon is holstered, as well as when the CPO has to draw the weapon.

Choice of holsters may have a large influence on this and many manuals recommend a holster with a retention clip for CPOs working in crowds since the clip would make it more difficult for an attacker in the crowd to remove the firearm from the holster while the extra time taken to draw the weapon is negligible. When considering the risks of the firearm being taken off an operative in such a situation, a holster designed to make a disarm more difficult would definitely be an advantage for a CPO.

Weapon integration skills

Depending on the threat level to a Principal, a CPO may need to have access to heavier weaponry than pistols (e.g., assault rifles, shotguns, etc.). In addition to such instances the CPO, if correctly trained, will be carrying alternative weaponry (such as batons and pepper sprays) and should be able to switch from weapon to weapon as the situation and use of force levels dictate.

The key competency when describing weapon integration skills is the ability to transition smoothly from one weapon to another while applying the applicable principles of close protection. This provides for contingencies that may occur and takes into account laws governing the use of force, as well as the guiding principle of limiting any harm occurring to innocent bystanders in crowded areas.

First Aid

A CPO needs to be able to provide not just emergency first aid, but also deal with any medical-related problems affecting his client until

The author demonstrating integration between handgun and tactical baton, while providing body cover.

more qualified medical assistance is available. Comprehensive first aid knowledge is vital for the protector in order to be able to perform all first aid-related duties that may be required by the Principal or his family.

Namely:

- Cardiopulmonary resuscitation
- Dealing with choking
- Dealing with wounds and bleeding

It is suggested that CPOs need to undergo more comprehensive first aid training, which would be done through external first aid training bodies such as the Red Cross or St John Ambulance Service.

Security and Planning

Trends can be summarized as follows:

Awareness and observation are fundamental functions of any close protection initiative and form the core of any security function.

Close protection specialists are constantly scanning the environment and applying effective awareness techniques to identify any potential threats or hazards and then take necessary action to avoid them.

Key Principles
_____

1. Consistently scan environment
2. Apply effective techniques
3. ID potential threats/hazards
4. Take necessary action to prevent

It would therefore make logical sense that most criminals, who are looking for easy victims would probably not target a person who was utilizing a close protection detail.

- In order to successfully plan security, effectively allocate resources and prevent attacks on the Principal the first step is to gather all necessary information in order to conduct a thorough risk and threat assessment.

- This happens together with a comprehensive principal profiling exercise. Principal profiling involves gathering as much information as possible on the Principal and formatting it into a workable structure to be used as an aid to determining a Principal's exposure to various threats and risks.

- A comprehensive risk analysis and threat assessment then needs to take place in order to determine the best manner in which to provide protection.

- Once you have these documents compiled, a summary of available resources must be collated. It is important at this stage to determine budgetary constraints and logistical considerations in order to maximize the use of resources to take place within a set budget.

- It is then a process of deciding how best to allocate resources according to the identified risks and threats and to minimize the potential of those threats happening.

Key Principles
_____

1. Allocate resources according to identified risks and threats

2. Minimize potential of threats happening

This must take place while planning around the Principal, taking into consideration such factors as his/her likes or dislikes and the need for the Principal to try and function with the minimum disruption to his or her routine or itinerary.

In order to gather the necessary information, analyze, collate, and structure that information into a practical format from which a comprehensive plan as well as the necessary contingency plans can be drawn up, the following aspects need to be not only understood but applied in the correct manner:

+ Understanding security as a whole
+ Basic intelligence collection and processing
+ Terrorism and assassination
+ Bomb and Identification of Explosive Devices (IED)
+ All threat analysis (obtaining all information and carefully analyzing it)
+ All risk assessments (obtaining all information and weighing up or assessing the analyzed information)
+ Surveillance and counter surveillance.

The above subjects form separate yet interrelated aspects of conducting a well-run security operation. It is important to stress that all these aspects must be viewed holistically and that, when applied, there is an intrinsic synergy in the way that each aspect enhances the manner in which the final planning is produced.

Protective Driving Skills

The concept of "defensive driving" is centered on identifying potential hazards before these pose a problem. The driver would than implement the necessary avoidance and management skills to ensure the safety and smooth journey of the passenger/Principal. It is vital that a CPO is a well-trained defensive driver, capable of recognizing and avoiding any potential collision before it occurs. Furthermore, a CPO must have all the necessary skills related to protective convoy and motorcade driving. These include all the necessary skills that would be applied when dealing with attack, surveillance and

For operations in a Third-World environment, training on dirt roads is a must.

29

ambush situations. Convoy driving refers to the tactics, practices, and application of formations utilized by a close protection detail when traveling with multiple vehicles. This is all done to successfully minimize the chance of attack on the Principal while in transit. Each of these will be explained in more detail below:

Defensive driving, as a CPO you must be able to:
Handle a vehicle in a safe and competent manner. It involves learning to preempt the mistakes that other drivers might make and take preventative action before they happen. The focus of defensive driving is being sufficiently aware to proactively identify any hazards in the environment with enough time to avoid or at the very least manage them. It is important to emphasize the vehicle control skills that are relevant under this heading such as managing skids, effective breaking procedures and emergency lane and direction changes. A CPO must at least be able to perform these skills to be considered competent.

Key Principles

1. Pre-empt hijackings
2. Take preventative action
3. Identify environmental hazards and manage them

Security awareness incorporated into preventative driving
This involves the integration of security concepts into defensive driving application. It means implementing the knowledge that a trained CPO should possess such as anti-ambush, sniping attacks, and vehicle security into everyday driving practice.

Key Principles

1. Anti-ambush
2. Hazard and route weak-point identification
3. Vehicle security

Convoy/motorcade driving
This is also often referred to as motorcade driving. This aspect describes the manner in which a Principal is transported when there are two or more vehicles available to provide protection. The methodology is designed to provide maximum security to the Principal by strategic positioning of the vehicles during all aspects of travel (stopping, cornering, intersections, etc.). This, combined with planned immediate action drills, should enable the convoy to effectively manage as many potential attacks and contingencies, in the most practical manner, while ensuring the Principal's safety.

Key Principles

1. Vehicle as a weapon
2. Shield
3. Evacuation

Offensive driving
Offensive driving refers to the techniques employed when utilizing the vehicle itself as

a weapon, shield or evacuation tool. It includes advanced handling, high speed driving, and the use of techniques such as handbrake and reverse turns to effectively avoid or engage an attacker.

Various manuals go into the topic of driving at different levels, but it is by nature a very practical subject. Therefore many of the important nuances cannot be found in the literature itself but only become apparent when interviewing close protection trainers and by observing the actual training (driving of vehicles) of CPOs.

Self Test

Name and describe 4 types of specialist driving skills

CPO Protocol and Etiquette

The aim of training in "protocol and etiquette" is to enable the CPO to conduct him/herself in a manner synonymous with the Principal and fitting for any situation or environment that the protector might find him/herself exposed to. The modern-day protector must be able to blend in at anything from ambassadorial house parties to a bush safari, etc. A CPO must be thoroughly versed in protocol to prevent embarrassment or discomfort to his/her Principal or other associated party.

The broad topic of protocol not only covers the obvious aspects of appearance and behavior but also goes deeper into the correct manner of liaison with various parties. Another factor to consider is the practical application of protocol—in other words, how protocol influences the CPO's ability to effectively protect the Principal and respond to attack situations if necessary.

It is vital that a CPO is able to relate to persons of different cultures and backgrounds, as the majority of persons utilizing CPOs are international. Protocol can be subdivided into the following areas:

- dress or appearance
- communication skills
- personal hygiene
- habits
- behavior
- social skills
- customs and traditions.

All of the above are important in order to develop sophisticated, professional, and well-rounded CPOs that can interact at any social level with their clients and Principals. Below, the basic requirements and skills for each subdivision are discussed in more detail.

Dress and appearance

The overall appearance of a CPO is vital to his/her ability to function in a professional manner. The Principal needs to be able to respect and trust his or her CPO. This is very difficult to do if the CPO does not look the part, is unhygienic and untidy, or does not dress suitably for the situation in which he/she is working. The CPO also needs to be able to blend into the immediate environment, i.e., not be conspicuous, and must therefore dress accordingly. The need to blend in is accentuated by the fact that the majority of close protection operations should be performed in a low-profile manner. A CPO not able to blend in would attract undue attention and therefore not be able to perform their duties very effectively, i.e., compromise the security of an assignment.

Key Principles
_____

1. Blend in
2. Don't draw attention
3. Don't compromise security of assignment

A key guideline for CPOs regarding dress and appearance would be to over-dress rather than under-dress as you can always dress down to blend into a situation but it does not necessarily work the other way around. Another consideration is that the CPO should attempt not to dress in a way that overshadows the Principal. The bottom line is that the CPO must dress appropriately for the situation and according to the Principal's wishes while still being able to react tactically if necessary (draw weapons, run or fight, etc.).

Communication skills

This concept includes much more than simply being able to verbally communicate with people. It involves all aspects of communication, namely verbal, non-verbal, written, and the subtle skill of utilizing body language to communicate. Much of a CPO's work will involve liaising with not only the Principal but also any person that can contribute to the success of an operation in any way.

Key Principle
_____

Verbalize requests in concise effective manner

Therefore, it is vital that the CPO is not only able to verbalize his/her requests in a concise and effective manner but is also able to relate to people of different cultures, backgrounds, and experience.

Personal hygiene

Even though the simple act of maintaining personal cleanliness and a professional appearance seems obvious, it is a topic that cannot be ignored. Due to the fact that a CPO may be mixing with people of high standing, it is essential for him/her to maintain a sufficient level of grooming to blend in and not attract undue attention to themselves or their Principal.

Habits

Habits refer to activities that are done so often that a person does not consciously realize that they are being performed. It goes without saying that good habits such as constant scanning and utilizing proactive awareness are vital for a CPO to carry out his or her job effectively. While positive habits are very important this section is primarily concerned with negative habits such as smoking or swearing.

Behavior

Behaviour primarily refers to the manner in which a CPO conducts him/herself when around the Principal. The idea is for the CPO to have the capability to behave in the correct manner in a wide variety of situations (social and business). For instance the CPO needs to know how to behave at embassy parties and in the business environment as well as when exposed to the Principal's private and family lifestyle. The better trained the CPO the more at ease he/she is in whatever the environment in which he/she must operate. This enables him/her to effectively perform the required protection duties without causing embarrassment to him/herself or the Principal.

It is equally important for a CPO to conduct him/herself "correctly" not only while working but all the time (i.e., even while off duty and in private life). The rationale behind this is that a CPO may be observed by clients while behaving inappropriately and might then not again be utilized by that client on operations in the future.

Self Test

Why is it important to behave appropriately at all times?

Social skills

A social skill refers to the way in which the CPO interacts with people in different environments. It also includes the correct etiquette involved when greeting people, the correct manner to eat in formal environments as well as the correct behavior when mixing with people of high standing. There are many guidelines for CPOs that fall under this heading. Some of the more generic concepts that apply here are concepts such as "when confused mirror the people around you" and "when unsure, rather be more formal in approach and language use."

Customs and traditions

It is vital for a professional CPO to have at least a rudimentary understanding of the customs and traditions of the different people that they may interact with during the course of performing close protection duties. **This is important since people may be offended by a CPO's actions without the CPO even realizing it.** Ignorance is not an excuse since once a person has been offended it may be difficult to undo the damage caused. This may cause embarrassment to the CPO and the Principal, as well as make any future interaction with the offended party difficult.

Customs and traditions can be classified into cultural, geographical, and religious categories and need to be researched, understood, and respected. It is a well-accepted fact by active members of the close protection industry that more CPOs lose their jobs over protocol- and etiquette-related transgressions than for any other reasons. This fact is easily explained, as a Principal will probably never see a CPO's hard skills ever being applied (shooting, tactical driving, unarmed combat, etc.) unless something goes drastically wrong during the protection assignment. Therefore, the interaction between the Principal and his protectors will be limited to the facets of protocol and etiquette as outlined above.

Self Test

Name the 7 aspects of protocol & etiquette and describe the main thinking behind each point

Written Field Work

Computer and Internet skills are a must for all CPOs. The ability to collate collected information and format it into usable documents that can be disseminated to all the parties that require the aforesaid information, is crucial for any professional CPO. The general written documents that are covered and explained in most literature are as follows:

Warning order

This is usually a short document drawn up before confirmation of an operation is received. The content of a warning order is usually verbally communicated to the relevant team members or may be passed on telephonically. The warning order serves as an indicator to the team members as to what may be expected of them, when it will take place, a brief overview of the Principal, and of the threats known at that stage. In other words, a warning order serves to alert CPOs to the basic details of a future assignment and that such an assignment is imminent.

An outline of what is going to happen next (order of proceedings) is usually included covering aspects such as the chain of command and relevant contact people. Because a warning order is often given verbally or telephonically specific details are often not included or pre-arranged code words are used.

Operational Appreciation – What do We Need to Effectively Run an Operation?

An Operational Appreciation is an activity designed to provide an overview of the situation and then enable the people planning an operation to determine what resources are needed and than allocate them effectively. The principal profile, the threat assessment and risk analysis, categorizing of the Principal and task, as well as determining what security should be implemented, all fall under the heading of Operational Appreciation.

Each of these are outlined below:

Threat assessments

There are several formats for threat and risk assessments that are identified. However, they generally seem to have four key components. The first component is the principal profile, which can be a stand-alone document and is explained in the next heading.

The second is a risk and threat analysis, which involves determining all the relevant threats that a Principal could be exposed to, and then correlating them with the principal profile to determine the risk factors (actual likelihood of an identified threat occurring). The next step is referred to as categorizing or designation of threats. This process involves several systems of analyzing the threat and risk as well as correlating these with the principal profile and Principal's proposed itinerary. The outcome of Principal categorization is to allocate the Principal and the operation (assignment) into a pre-defined category.

Key Principles

1. Determine all relevant threats
2. Correlate with Principal profile

The classifications into various categories can get quite complex but as a simple overview the Principal and operation could be grouped into a low-threat, medium-threat or high-threat category. Each of these would involve different logistical and operational requirements. This last aspect involves deciding on the security and way that it will be applied in order to minimize the likelihood of the defined threat and risks occurring or at the very least minimizing the effects of the threat should it occur.

3 Levels of Threat

- Low
- Medium
- High

Principal profiling

It is impossible to plan for an effective close protection initiative if nothing is known about the Principal. There are several systems and methods used to profile the Principal. Profiling in its simplest form is an attempt to find out as much as possible about a Principal in order to determine what sort of person they are and what factors linked to his/her persona might impact on the safety and security of the close protection operation. In the close protection context, this is vital, since not knowing relevant information about the Principal could lead to the unwitting exposure to threats that could have been avoided or planned for. In addition, when referring to the definition of Close Protection it would be almost impossible to ensure the Principal's peace of mind and comfort if nothing is known about his/her likes and dislikes.

In order to provide the reader with a better understanding of the concept of principal profiling, a method commonly utilized known as the "seven Ps of principal profiling" will be described. The fundamental concept is that under each heading as much relevant information regarding the Principal as possible should be collected. This information will then be sorted and classified before being converted into the final format.

Self Test

Name the 7 Ps
of principal profiling

The seven Ps of principal profiling are as follows:

1. **Places**
   All the places associated with the Principal, i.e., where he/she likes to go, where they work, live, and play.
2. **People**
   The many people that are related to, associated with or at some time or other have interacted with the Principal.
3. **Political and religious persuasions**
   The relevant political and religious persuasions of the Principal, as well as associated places that the Principal attends
4. **Prejudices**
   What the Principal likes and dislikes (e.g., extreme dislike for people that smoke).
5. **Personal history**
   Where the Principal has been and what he/she has done to get to where he/she is now.
6. **Private Lifestyle**
   What the Principal does in his/her spare time including recreational activities, hobbies, and pastimes, e.g., hiking, sports, gym, movies, theatres, restaurants, etc.
7. **Personality**
   What sort of personality characteristics the Principal exhibits, e.g., quiet and withdrawn, outspoken and extroverted, etc.

Once all this information has been collected, it can then be analyzed—eliminating what may be considered superfluous or not relevant to the specific task at hand. The process would then be to transform the information into a workable document to assist in operational planning and the briefing of the operational team.

Operations order

An Operations Order (Ops Order) is the finalized document outlining the who, what, when, why, and how of a close protection operation. It should provide as much information as possible, including the operation specific Standard Operating Procedures (SOPs). The Ops Order should be detailed enough to cover most of the contingencies that may occur. It should also cover any additional information concerning protocol, dress, communications, and logistical information.

Self Test

What is an operations order?

Record and report keeping

In most situations, each operative would submit a report at the end of each operation or segment of an operation. The procedure for this would be outlined in the Ops Order's SOPs. After receiving each CPO's report, the team leader would prepare a comprehensive operational report that could serve as feedback for the client. Another benefit of receiving feedback and compiling an operational report is that it provides a platform for the review of mistakes that may have occurred. It also provides an opportunity to clarify how such mistakes can be avoided in the future, what the successes were and how to maintain and even enhance them if possible. Information documents should then be duplicated and stored in a secure environment, as information gathered and lessons learned may very well be applied on future operations even if the operation is not with the same Principal. Secure storage of documents is vital—should the information obtained in these documents fall into the wrong hands it would be relatively easy to plan an attack on future Principals.

Once again, it is important to note the way that technology is influencing the approach to compiling these documents and formatting them into information databases, which can easily be accessed and utilized in future operations. Accordingly, a modern CPO should, as a matter of course, be at least reasonably computer literate and be proficient in the use of basic computer programs and how to safeguard all this classified information on computer systems and computer files, so that they can't be accessed.

Related Skills (Operational Appreciation & Management)

Hostage crisis and management

This subject refers to the accepted operating procedures that apply to hostage situations and the role that a CPO will play should the Principal and/or him/herself be taken hostage. The following key aspects are outlined:

1. Negotiation techniques
2. Hostage survival
3. Stress identification and coping
4. Escape and evasion.

Anti- and counter-terrorism

The topic of terrorism is covered in almost every training manual but in varying detail. Certain literature however, goes into much greater depth than others by outlining the roles and duties that would be necessary to implement in order to prevent acts of terrorism from taking place (anti-terrorism) and how to manage and deal with terrorist attacks and situations that may occur (counter-terrorism). It should be noted that while a CPO may not need comprehensive anti- or counter-terrorist training he/she should, at the very least, have a basic knowledge of terrorist activity. Most manuals include notes and background information on the following aspects of terrorism:

1. Terrorist groups
2. Terrorist selection and training
3. General modus operandi
4. Effects of terrorism on security and close protection.

The author kitted up for CAT training. Visible equipment includes:
• Long weapon
• Tactical baton
• Pepper spray.

Not visible: Sidearm, spare magazines, tactical torch, radio and combat folder knife.

Counter-sniping

Counter-sniping is also referred to as selective tactical marksmanship. This subject could also be placed in the section on firearms training (dealt with later). In order to employ counter-sniping principles it is important to know the fundamentals of sniping. This is taught and explained in order for CPOs to know how to implement counter measures and plan against a sniping attack.

Specialized tactical training

Some of these skills would be more applicable when the training of Counter Action Teams (CAT) is considered. It was also stated that if there was a high enough threat level to warrant the use of a person with the skills below, they could be subcontracted and brought in to assist on a temporary basis. More comprehensive tactical training may include some of the following aspects:

- rope work (rappelling and abseiling, use of ropes to gain access or egress to a structure)
- foreign weapons training (if operating abroad where the weapons may be different to what the CPO is trained to use, this specialized knowledge could be important)
- team tactics
- parachuting
- scuba diving
- survival training in different environments.

Waterborne security

The concepts behind application of "waterborne security" as it relates to close protection refers to providing security and ensuring the safety of a Principal while on any waterborne craft, e.g., yachts, speed boats, ocean liners, etc. This may involve the CPO being trained in some of the following:

- scuba diving
- life-saving techniques
- sea survival.

There is extensive literature available on theses topics but for the purposes of this book, it is enough that the relevance of the link to close protection is identified and understood.

Aviation security

Aviation security refers to the necessary security measures that need to be implemented when a Principal is traveling via aircraft. Most experts seems to agree that due to the complexity of modern aircraft it is almost impossible for a CPO to do an effective search of an airplane (for any signs of sabotage of the plane itself) without the hands-on assistance of a pilot and mechanic. In most cases, unless the Principal has their own aircraft, this topic is not necessary for CPOs and would be limited to the vetting of the airline that the Principal chooses to fly on. Within the context of recent terrorist threats, it would also include an evaluation of the airline not only on safety record but also on current threat levels, as well as the perceived risk of a terrorist group targeting that specific airline. More comprehensive training in this topic could include training in:

+ aircraft search procedures
+ parachuting
+ emergency procedures, i.e., evacuation and crash procedures.

The field of aviation security is a specialist field in its own right and if it was deemed relevant, it would be more logical for a CPO to utilize the services of an expert in the field than attempt to learn all the necessary skills.

Information Security

Information security refers to all relevant aspects that control access to information on the Principal, his/her movements, business interests, and personal life. The increasing importance of this topic as it relates to close protection means that even though this aspect could have been included in several other broader topics as a subfield, it is not. This is perhaps because it is a specialized field into itself and the ease of access to information through modern technology (the Internet) has made the need for information security even more pertinent. As a result, the research has shown that it should receive its own separate section to ensure that it is covered in the necessary detail. The field of information security can be broken down into the following areas:

+ intelligence gathering
+ surveillance and counter-surveillance
+ document security
+ IT/computer security

Certain key concepts are universal when security as a whole is evaluated but are even more relevant when referring to close protection. Some of these are concepts such as "need to know" and restriction of access to sensitive information. Once again, this topic and its relevant subdivisions constitute a specialist field in its own right.

With modern technology and specialist surveillance equipment (bugs, high-resolution cameras, etc.) becoming so advanced, it may be almost impossible to locate such devices using only a hand-eye search. If threats at this level are identified it is necessary to employ the services of competent electronic counter measures (ECM) professionals that have the relevant sophisticated equipment and experience to locate such devices.

Conclusion – Summary of Key Points

The primary aim of this chapter is to serve as a foundation for the chapters that follow. These chapters will relate the above theoretical breakdown into a practical format by analyzing feedback from research conducted by interviewing specialists in their relevant fields.

As can be seen from the many topics and subjects mentioned above, modern-day Close Protection is a comprehensive discipline. It requires its operatives to not only have the necessary hard skills to perform the work but also possess the soft skills needed to keep the client satisfied and prevent potential embarrassment to the Principal by blending into the environment.

The breakdown above is in no way a recommended training format but simply provides a framework from which to explain all the relevant aspects that combine to make an effective and professional CPO. Many of the topics outlined in this chapter are re-examined in more detail later in this book.

CHAPTER 4

How to Select the Right Trainer & the Best Training Program for You

*"I hear and I forget,
I see and I remember,
I do and I understand"*
—Confucius

Introduction

The role of the close protection operative may involve the application of many different operational skills. In order for a CPO to gain these skills, he/she needs to complete a comprehensive training program. This training can be explained in a three-step process, namely:

1. Training is the ongoing process of learning and developing skills
2. It is also the gaining of the relevant theoretical and background knowledge
3. It is undergone in order to ensure that the skills and knowledge can be applied in practice.

In many cases this training process would often have to occur under duress, since effective training should prepare students for the actual situations where they would have to apply what they have learned, i.e., simulate the conditions of real-life situations.

As far as close protection is concerned the field of necessary skills and knowledge in its entirety is very broad. This is so because almost any aspect or subfield of security could be considered relevant to close protection.

A comprehensive initial training course should be considered as the starting point for almost any CPO's career. It would be fair to say that a CPO's initial training would probably determine operational practices for the rest of that CPO's career.

The importance of ongoing training and retraining is also a vital training component if a CPO is to remain at a level of operational proficiency. It is important to determine what CPOs should actually be able to do and at what level, they should be able to do it, in order to be considered competent.

The themes and points associated with close protection training can be identified as:

+ Screening of candidates before training or pre-selection
+ The duration of training
+ The intensity of training
+ The content of training
+ The focus of training
+ Regulatory aspects and standards related to training

Each of the aspects mentioned above will be unbundled and explained later in this chapter.

Can Close Protection be Divided According to Tasks and Competencies?

CPOs need to be multi-skilled. With more experience and training, a CPO with the correct attributes should develop into a team leader. This approach demonstrates that there is chain of command in place and the possibility of job progression.

> *"A CPO must be able to perform all relevant duties. He [she] may be a specialist in a certain field but should be able to operate in any function on a team."*
> — David M. Sharp

It is also possible to subdivide the roles and duties according to competency and task. The following generic subdivisions illustrate how the division, according to task (these are expanded below):

1. Static protector
2. Security driver
3. CPO
4. Team leader
5. Group/operational leader

Static protector

A static protector is an individual working as part of a larger team providing protection at a venue or a residence. He/she would perform these duties whether a Principal was at the venue or not. People providing static duties do not move around with the Principal and have very little personal interaction with him/her. In most cases, this would be considered the starting point for a CPO's career.

Security driver

A security driver would be a person trained in both security and driving skills. His/her primary responsibility would be to facilitate the smooth transfer of the Principal from venue to venue. A security driver's roles and duties would not extend to actually walking around with the Principal or protecting the venues that the Principal was visiting. A slightly different mix of competencies is necessary for a person to perform either static or security driver functions. A driver would obviously need driving skills but must also have a well-developed sense of protocol. This is vital as in some cases a security driver would be alone in the car with the Principal.

Close protection operative

A CPO is a security specialist who has been trained to provide the maximum possible protection in any given circumstance. The most common breakdown would be to provide protection while a Principal is static, at a venue or his/her residence, in transit or on foot. A CPO must be able to operate as an individual or member of a team. By definition, a CPO should be able to perform all the necessary tasks of both a security driver and a static protector.

Team leader

A team leader is a person who is able to coordinate the running of a close protection team. He/she should be thoroughly versed in the planning, transit, venue, foot, and debrief aspects of a close protection operation. The team leader should also have more developed communication, managerial, and leadership skills than a CPO. A team leader should have at least three years of operational experience, show a natural flair for leadership and perhaps undergo additional training focusing on subjects like communication, management, leadership, and administration.

Group/operational leader

An operational leader would usually have been a CPO who has experience as a team leader and is considered capable of coordinating several close protection teams at the same time. A group leader should have at least two years experience working as a team leader as well as undergo additional management-skills training programs.

Screening of Candidates Before Training (Pre-selection)

The relevant aspects with which a prospective CPO candidate should be able to comply with are outlined below (in no particular order of preference):

- Should not have a criminal record
- Should pass a full medical examination and a basic fitness evaluation test
- Should possess a valid drivers license
- Have a suitable level of both literacy and numeric skills
- Demonstrate an ability to cope well with stress and fatigue
- Experience with firearms, martial arts is useful
- Previous experience in private security, police, military or other related agencies is an advantage.

Duration of Training

The duration of training refers to the period necessary to train a person from totally unskilled to the level of a competent CPO. While ongoing training and retraining are key considerations when discussing time frames, they will be discussed in a later section of this chapter.

During the research for this book, experts who were interviewed gave feedback on training course duration. The suggested periods have been correlated from the expert's feedback and divided accordingly into two different schools of thought, namely, whether a CPO has to be trained in all aspects or can be trained in specific aspects of a CPO.

Training course periods vary and are largely based on such factors as course content, time worked per day and number of students per course (student-to-instructor ratio). Many experts firmly believe that before a prospective CPO could be said to be competent he/she should undergo an apprentice (in-service training) period where he/she would be supervised and guided by an experienced operative.

The relevant time frames will be discussed below. (For the sake of uniformity, the number of days, not weeks, is used as the measuring tool for duration. Eight hours of training was considered one day.)

Fully competent CPO

The average accepted duration for a candidate to achieve the necessary competence in the required operational skills of close protection is 20–30 days. This was based on including a short (either full-day or half-day) student selection and vetting process prior to the commencement of training. It was also worth noting that advanced training programs could be developed that would enhance the CPO's skills and knowledge that were imparted in the initial training.

Subdivision of roles and duties

The most logical approach to the training of CPOs in the various subdivisions of close protection is to look at this method (training according to role and duty) of training in a progressive manner. In other words, once a candidate has completed the skills requirements for static, transit, and foot protection, he/she would have fulfilled the requirements to operate as a fully competent CPO (as above). Each of the previously mentioned task subdivisions has been given a training duration (as explained below).

The initial starting point for a prospective CPO would be to qualify as a static protector (a static protector is the starting point for training a CPO in a subdivided manner). Once qualified as a static protector the prospective CPO would then undergo training to qualify as a security driver. It would not really make a difference whether a potential CPO qualified as a security driver or static protector first. The recommended training period for each of these close protection aspects was estimated to be 7–10 days.

In order for a candidate to then further qualify as a CPO, he/she will have to undergo additional training in the provision of close protection to a Principal while on foot. The recommended training time frame for protection on foot is also 7–10 days. This would mean that for a new student to qualify as a fully competent CPO, he/she would have to undergo an overall training period of 21–30 days (much the same as a full time CPO course).

Intensity of Training Courses

The concept of intensity refers not only to the duration of training each day but also to the level of physical, emotional and psychological stress that is placed on the candidate during the training, as well as the detail of the course content.

Several experts are of the opinion that training candidates at a consistently high intensity is actually the best way to produce the most competent CPOs. The quote below highlights this concept:

> "When the focus of the training is to produce 'Special
> Forces type' operatives [CPOs], much of the point may be
> missed, as the students are not actually being trained to do
> the job [of close protection]
> that they will have to perform"
> —Clinton McGuire

Moreover, other relevant factors that were discussed during some interviews with experts focused on the skills progression of students, while they undergo training. Issues such as the logical progression of training, as well as the focus on training the prospective CPO for the actual job requirements of close protection, as opposed to the perceived requirements are amongst factors to be noted. It is vital that the training builds up progressively to a point where the realities of the close protection world are experienced by trainees.

Some of these would include aspects such as little sleep, irregular eating patterns and monotonous periods of time followed by frantic activity, team interaction and coping with frustration while staying alert.

It is possible (but not recommended) to train CPOs in a shorter time frame, i.e., 10–12 days providing that the intensity is high. Training time would be approximately 15 or 16 hours a day (the number of hours is not necessarily shorter but more hours of training are crammed into less days). If this approach is taken then the CPO should have to spend time undergoing an apprenticeship and be mentored and monitored by a more experienced CPO.

For training based on applicable competencies to be successfully presented in this book, it must be assumed that candidates have undergone a pre-selection evaluation and posses all the preferred attributes (these attributes will be discussed later in this book) of a CPO. In other words, for shortened training to be effective, the candidate needs to be almost perfect for job (physically and mentally) before training starts.

Content of Training Courses

Content refers to the actual subject matter that is taught to the students during a close protection training course. For the purposes of this book, content will be grouped according to its nature into either being theoretically or practically based. A common concern expressed by several experts, is that much of the theory taught on close protection training programs is either irrelevant or did not relate to what was actually done in practice.

Furthermore, another area of concern mentioned in several interviews was that the content in many close protection training programs was not reality based. In the in-depth interviews, experts were first asked to identify what they considered, in order of importance, to be the required operational skills a CPO should possess in order to effectively perform his/her duties. They were then asked to explain what training a person would have to undergo in order to be able to meet the skills requirements that they had just identified.

Based on the expert's replies, two basic key grouping criteria for skills requirements could be identified, namely:

1. Personal attributes and personality traits

Certain of the skills requirements were based on physical attributes and appearance, and others on psychological or personality characteristics. Most of these cannot actually be taught (not a learned skill), however if a candidate did have them, even on a rudimentary level, these could most probably be developed.

2. Learned skills

The relevant CPO skills that can be taught are skills consistent with almost any close protection training program that was examined when researching this book. What differs between various training programs is the focus and time spent on each aspect (focus will be discussed in the next section). Several experts believe that content could be divided into different levels of candidate proficiency (e.g., basic, intermediate, and advanced). This is, in itself, a controversial issue as experts differed in their opinion on whether you could subdivide the competencies required of CPOs at all. Certain experts stated that there is no such thing as basic level since a CPO is either competent or not (he/she can either protect somebody effectively or cannot).

However, even if this argument is applied, it still leaves room for higher levels of proficiency over and above what can be considered the minimum level of competency for a CPO. The wide scope of subject matter that would fit into the "nice to have" and "related skills" categories are almost endless. Therefore, a CPO could constantly be expanding his/her knowledge base of close protection related knowledge and skills.

The Focus of Close Protection Training

It would make sense that the focus of training should be on the subjects that would be vital for performance of effective CPO duties. One of the primary identified problems is that even though most experts agreed on the basic subjects that would fall into this category, they differed on the focus that should be given to each aspect. These differences were mainly on the amount of time that should be spent on each aspect, the detail at which the subject should be taught and what could be considered the level of competency for each subject.

By correlating information collected from the research, several key focus areas are identified. Overall, it is not possible to say that one aspect is more important than another. Rather the approach should be that all aspects are interdependent and that each is vital for the effective performance of close protection duties. In other words, an integrated and interlinked training program would be the ideal, where multiple skills support and supplement each other to develop a well-rounded (holistic), multi-skilled CPO.

Some of the key focus points that are identified in this book as being vital to ensure a well-rounded training program can be outlined as follows:

- Practical application of close protection theory including knowledge of all legalities involved in the provision of close protection
- Ensuring the trainee has the ability to cope with fatigue, stress, boredom, and adverse working conditions through reality-based training scenarios and an intense training regime
- Ensuring that a trainee is taught all physical skills (fitness, unarmed combat, use of alternative weaponry, firearms, and driving skills)
- Basic first aid skills
- Ability to work as an individual or member of a team
- Development of trainee attributes such as commitment, aggression and determination
- Soft skills such as protocol, people skills, and liaison ability
- Determination of the trainee's integrity and trustworthiness through scenario-based training.

Training should ideally, therefore, focus on the development of the above-mentioned skills and attributes in a practical, work environment related manner. It would be fair to state that if a CPO was found particularly lacking in one of the above aspects, he/she would probably not be performing the relevant duties as effectively as they should be. Moreover, another problem is that the only time a client actually gets to see whether a CPO is capable of performing the necessary life-saving and protection skills is when things have gone completely wrong (lack of planning, poor protocol or even an attack situation). At this stage, a CPO's lack of rounded competencies could potentially cost a Principal and members of the close protection team their lives, or at best, the CPO company would lose the contract (i.e., not get more business from that specific client).

Ongoing Training and Retraining

Retraining can be explained as an ongoing process of repetition, restudy, rehearsal and performance of skills that a trained CPO has already been exposed to. Ongoing training can be explained as the process of gaining new knowledge and/or skills covering as many factors and aspects that are applicable to the performance of CPO and related duties. In the in-depth interviews experts were first asked whether they felt retraining and ongoing training were necessary. If they answered yes, they were then asked what format such retraining and ongoing training should take, as well as how often it should take place.

Experts are of the opinion that retraining is vital and that ongoing training should be done. Furthermore, the focus of such training should be on the long-term career development of a CPO and not just on skills maintenance. The main reasons mentioned for the importance of retraining were two-fold. Firstly, many of the physical skills are "perishable," meaning that if they are not practiced regularly the ability to perform them effectively diminishes. Moreover, many of these skills may have to be performed under extreme stress and duress, i.e., pressure situations. This means that in order for a CPO to be able to perform under such conditions, there must be regular exposure to similar type situations. The safest way to do this is through reality-based retraining.

The second reason identified was simply that CPOs would usually, over a period of time, forget what they had learned during their initial training. This is especially true for those aspects of protection that may not be applied in the everyday working environment. This could also be attributed to the wide subject base that should be covered during initial training.

Frequency of retraining

Several experts have differing opinions about how often retraining should be run, saying that retraining should take place as often as possible and that a CPO should do some sort of physical training daily. Others suggest different approaches such as, allocating two weeks a year for a relatively thorough close protection retraining course (refresher). In this case, it was mentioned that it was the individual CPO's responsibility to maintain fundamental physical skills and fitness levels. A realistic approach would most probably be a combination of the two opinions.

Ideally the individual CPO should maintain adequate fitness levels on his/her own, with group and team training (e.g., repetitive drills) taking place whenever possible but at least once a month. Longer training workshops can be run once or twice a year.

These longer sessions could last for a few days and cover a wider range of relevant skills and topics as well as serving as a forum to update the CPO on new methods, tactics, etc. Such a format would allow for retraining that would keep the necessary skills at an effective level of competency as well as provide a platform for ongoing training during group and longer bi-annual sessions. An extra bonus to retraining is that it serves as a team building mechanism to develop trust, build confidence in each other's skills and competencies as well as create a bond between a team of CPOs.

The focus of retraining

The focus of the retraining, as previously mentioned, should concentrate on perishable skills. These would primarily be those skills that a CPO would not utilize in his/her everyday work but which are vital if an attack on the Principal were to take place. These skills can be divided into one of the following broad categories:

- Everyday working skills (driving, communication, protocol, etc.)
- Management of attack situations (unarmed combat, firearms skills, IADs, etc.)
- First aid and reactive skills (CPR, Principal evacuations, crisis management, etc.)
- Physical fitness and related skills (strength, stamina, agility, etc.).

Retraining should focus on maintaining all competencies in each of the above categories. A combination of individual and group training is necessary to cover all relevant aspects of the above subdivisions. As one of the respondents put it, "retraining should be done as often as a protector's work schedule permits. It is very important for a CPO to stay sharp."

Instructor-Related Factors

An aspect of concern that was raised by several experts during the interviews was that they felt that close protection training was not always as effective as it should be. The most common reasoning for this phenomenon was attributed, not so much to the training content, but rather to incompetent instructors and ineffective methods of instruction.

What Makes Someone a Competent Instructor

It was universally accepted that the quality and credentials of instructors is very important, if CPOs are to be able to operate at a high standard. Instructor credentials and monitoring was mentioned by experts from both service and civilian backgrounds alike as a problem in the industry. On analysis of the problem, two related aspects were identified as probable causes for any close protection instructor-related problems. These were either the instructors possibly not having the necessary operational experience to train candidates effectively and/or they were not trained in effective instructional methodology (teaching skills).

A solution to this problem is relatively simple to identify, namely to implement a regulatory system and standards enforcement approach for instructors in order to ensure a high-quality level of training. This approach would have to be twofold. Firstly, ensure that instructors receive training on how to instruct (train-the-trainer program). Secondly, verify that potential instructors have actually had experience in the close protection field (background checks). Problems with this approach would probably hinge on the implementation and enforcement of instructor regulation.

In order to implement a system of instructor regulation, minimum standards (for an instructor's credentials and qualifications) have to be identified and set levels of competency (teaching skills) implemented, as well as quantifying how much experience instructors actually need to have in order to be considered qualified to train. A guideline approach is outlined below:

1. Complete a **generic assessors' course** (a course that teaches how to assess competency)
2. The registration should include evaluation of the candidate's resume and prior experience in order to establish if he/she has the necessary credentials to be considered a **Subject Matter Expert** (SME).
3. In order to qualify as a trainer the candidate would have to undergo a train-the-trainer course or relevant teaching/training qualification (for example, in Australia the candidate would need to complete a Certificate Course in training and assessment)

For an instructor to deliver training in the private sector, he/she should have to operate through an accredited training provider. In order for a company or individual to be accredited, they should have to undergo an extensive accreditation process. This process would ensure that a provider has the ability to offer high-quality training and maintain effective records of such training. As an example: the accreditation process in South Africa includes a verification of service provider details and infrastructure, an assessment of the providers' quality management system, learning materials, policies and procedures, and an evaluation of all training venues available to such a company or individual. To maintain accreditation the SASSETA requires updates on all of the aspects just mentioned, as well as the right to inspect training and operations at their sole discretion.

Instructional Methodology Needed for Close Protection Training

Instructional methodology refers to the manner in which the relevant information and skills are conveyed from trainer to trainee. The focus of this concept is now leaning heavily towards outcomes-based education (OBE). The fundamental concepts of OBE are based on the learner gaining an understanding of the rationale behind why things are done and on actual application of knowledge acquired. This differs from other approaches where students may have to learn by memorizing facts and concepts.

Some other key concepts of OBE that are applicable to close protection training are directly linked to adult-based education and training (ABET), which focuses on the practical and measurable outcomes of training. The concepts of ABET would definitely be applicable to close protection training since, in most cases, the recommended minimum age for candidates would be around 21. One of the focuses of ABET is to relate new concepts to already existing knowledge or experiences that the candidates may have had. This is effective, as candidates will learn faster by relating new concepts to knowledge that they may already have, it would be important for training methodology to concentrate on expanding on students' existing knowledge and competency base.

When considering the need for practical measurable outcomes, many experts believe that it is vital for outcomes to be in line with the performance of close protection duties in the work environment. Additionally, "fundamental [close protection] work competencies should always take precedence over a CPO's 'nice to have skills.'" This concept is important as a CPO must keep his/her client happy and, of course, safe. It should be mentioned that even though the vast majority of close protection tasks do not always amount to a CPO actually having to utilize his/her combat related skills, it is vital to remember that a CPO is primarily employed to protect a Principal's life and well-being. A CPO would not be able to do this without a solid base of effective combat-related skills.

NB! Experts indicate that they feel training should be provided in such a way as to imitate (simulate) the actual conditions within which CPOs need to operate This idea would be in contravention of many of the training doctrines applied in training for other jobs. Some of these training doctrines emphasize that a trainee should be comfortable, in a well-organized environment that is free from distractions in order for learning to take place. This "simulated training" picks up on the concept of experiential learning, i.e., on-the-job training. While both theoretical and practical skills are important in order for a CPO to provide effective protection, his/her ability to actually "do the job" is what counts the most.

NB! It should be noted that Close Protection work is not for everyone and if during training a trainee cannot cope with stress, lack of sleep, discomfort, and other job-related factors, he/she is actually the wrong person for the job. Instructional methodology should therefore concentrate on training candidates for the job they are going to have to do. This should include all the stress and duress factors related to close protection operations. The instructor should also concentrate on an outcomes-based approach that relates prior experi-

ences of trainees to what they need to learn. This approach of adult-based education and training is important to enable students to have the maximum possible understanding of close protection methodology.

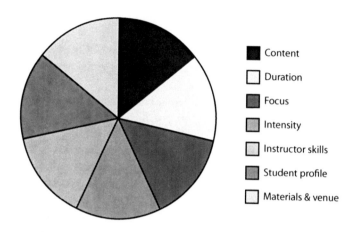

Chart 1: Variables needed for effective close protection training.

Legend:
- Content
- Duration
- Focus
- Intensity
- Instructor skills
- Student profile
- Materials & venue

Conclusion – Summary of Key Points

Training is vital for a CPO to operate and perform effectively in the work environment. Various fundamental aspects related to close protection training were identified during the research for this book. These include concepts such as the intensity, focus, content, and duration of training programs. Other key areas of concern that were identified are aspects pertaining to instructor credentials and the instructor's ability to deliver the training in an effective manner.

Furthermore, other relevant aspects that were related to training of CPOs and which were consistently mentioned in the in-depth interviews included concepts such as:

- Prospective candidates for CPO training should undergo a pre-selection (including a background check, physical and psychological suitability assessments, etc.) prior to the commencement of training. This pre-evaluation would be used to determine whether the candidate has the correct profile to be a CPO.
- Ensuring training prepares students for the actual job they must perform and is not presented based on the instructor's preconceived ideas of what he/she believes to be the most important aspects of close protection.

- The applied training methodology must shift to focus on outcomes-based education and capitalize on the use of adult-based education techniques.
- Training conditions (lack of sleep, induced stress, etc.) should simulate the pressure and work environment of an actual close protection operation.
- Retraining should be an integral part of any CPO's operational life. He/she should regularly attend ongoing training sessions and refresher workshops.
- CPOs should attempt to implement as much additional and ongoing training, whenever possible, to facilitate career advancement.

There were also instructor-related issues that are identified as having a major influence on the effectiveness of training. Some of the key aspects regarding instructors and instructional methodology were:

- The fact that instructors should be CPOs with valid and appropriate field experience. This is important to ensure that trainees benefit from the instructor's hands-on experience.
- It is necessary for potential close protection instructors to undergo training in instructional methodology. The instructor should have a recognized trainer's (instructor's) qualification and posses a valid Assessors certification before being allowed to present courses.
- The information provided indicates that in order for training to be effective and efficient, the above considerations need to be addressed. Additionally the regulation of instructors and training providers should be enforced in order to maintain high standards.

CHAPTER 5

PERCEPTIONS ABOUT CLOSE PROTECTION

"Most of the mistakes in thinking are inadequacies of perception rather than mistakes of logic."
—Edward de Bono

Introduction

A perception could be described as something that a person or group of persons may believe to be reality. A problem with someone's perceptions is that they may not be founded on fact and experience but rather on what seems to be the most convenient, well received or widely disseminated idea. This may also be true for persons superimposing their perceptions on reality in order to create a platform of concepts that make sense to them.

Perception, in close protection terms, would not only affect almost all aspects of training but also the way in which CPOs actually provide protection. This could be dangerous for if a CPO were to react to a perceived threat and not a real threat, the consequences could be potentially life threatening or at the least very embarrassing for the CPO and the Principal. Research has indicated that there are many misconceptions about close protection.

Additionally, there appears to be an overall lack of understanding regarding the core roles and responsibilities of CPOs by the general public, the security industry and regulatory bodies. Several perception-related inaccuracies were identified. These include concepts such as: who is actually qualified to be a CPO, what a qualified CPO should be capable of doing and how he/she should actually perform close protection.

Key Principle

The need to identify the realities of close protection as opposed to perception

This crucial concept has much bearing in determining the necessary operational skills requirements needed to provide effective close protection. This is especially relevant when considering the perceptions of clients, other security providers and trainers. The need to identify the realities of close protection as opposed to perceptions is vital in order to determine the correct profile, skills requirements, and steps required to implement an effective client education program about close protection.

Furthermore, this doubles up and affects not only CPO duty, but also training because if the realities of the above aspects are not identified and determined, it would be almost impossible to develop an outcomes-based training program that would be orientated to the actual job description of a CPO. A recurring theme that was identified in interviews with experts was that CPOs should be trained according to the actual tasks that are to be performed while operating. This should supersede those aspects that may have been defined as "nice to have" skills.

A major contributing factor to inaccurate perceptions mentioned by most experts was the influence of the media's portrayal of CPOs. Movies such as *The Bodyguard* and *In the Line of Fire* have created a distorted image of CPOs and what they do. At first glance, the portrayal of CPOs and their work may appear to be real, but when looking closer it can be easily discerned that these films are focusing on the entertainment value of close protection as opposed to an accurate portrayal of the CPO and his/her duties.

In this chapter, aspects such as the profiling, the preferred characteristics of CPOs in terms of physical appearance and personality will be examined. The identified core skills requirements will also be discussed.

CPO Profiles

The profile of a CPO would include, but not be limited to, those physical and personality characteristics and the learned skills that contribute to his/her ability to effectively perform all the necessary duties of close protection provision. **It is vital to differentiate between what the perceived realities are and what is actually relevant to clients and operatives in the industry.**

On analysis, the physical characteristics of CPOs could be unpacked into the following broad subdivisions:

+ appearance
+ build
+ attributes.

Personality characteristics would refer to those behavioral and subconscious tendencies that dictate a CPO's behavior in different circumstances. Lastly, learned skills would go hand-in-hand with a potential CPO's natural ability to absorb and perform the skills, physical and mental, necessary to perform the different aspects of close protection.

Physical Characteristics of CPOs

Physical appearance

When analyzing what a CPO should look like, it is best to refer back to the initial job description of a CPO, discussed earlier in this book. This would infer that a CPO who is responsible for the safety, peace of mind, and physical comfort of his/her Principal should be physically capable of carrying out all activities necessary to achieve these goals. This, however, goes a step further as we need to take into consideration the Principal's profile as well as the applicable risk and threat. It is vital to consider these variables prior to determining what the CPO should look like in a given situation. This is important, as the CPO must be physically suited to the task at hand.

There are several factors which come into play when analyzing the correct physical appearance of a CPO. These include the Principal's profile, his/her personal preferences, and the environment in which the job is to take place. The identified threat and risks need always to be taken into account.

> *A CPO is not a bouncer, he/she should be of*
> *normal appearance [not have distinguishing*
> *(i.e., standout) physical characteristics] and be capable*
> *of blending into almost any environment*
> —David M. Sharp

The author and CP team awaiting the arrival of a Principal.
(Note the CPO in the background covering the rear of the area behind the jet.)

The author deployed on operations in East Africa.
(Note the difference in dress from the picture on previous page;
a CPO must dress according to the environment.)

The concept of a CPO being able to blend into his/her environment may be dependent on certain physical characteristics. Some of these will be outlined below.

1. A CPO working in the corporate environment should not be too heavily built and should be able to blend into many different environments within which he/she might have to operate, i.e., be inconspicuous and not stand out in a crowd.

2. A CPO must be able to apply the correct protocol and dress according to any situation to assist them in blending in.

3. A CPO should be in such physical condition so as to have a professional appearance yet be capable of performing all related protection duties, i.e., not overweight, unfit, too young or old.

Furthermore, it should be noted that the profile of the operation, as well as the environment wherein the operation is occurring, would determine what the physical appearance of a CPO should be. The common theme identified from the research for this book was that protection should remain as low profile as possible (i.e., low-key and not attract unwanted attention). In other words, the CPO must not draw attention to him/herself by dress, behavior or mannerisms. The reasoning behind this is that it is possible to go from a low-profile operation to a visible and obvious high profile, but the converse is not always possible. Therefore, utilizing a close protection team that would attract attention purely because of their physical appearance would not be considered the preferred option.

However, it should be mentioned that it may be advantageous to utilize CPOs with different physical characteristics based on the environmental factors and operational demands of a task. Should the protection detail be operating extensively in crowds providing protection for a high-profile Principal, it may be wise to utilize physically large "bouncer-type" CPOs. This would not only assist in the intimidation of the crowd but would also make the evacuation of a Principal easier should it be required.

It would therefore be fair to state that in the vast majority of close protection related situations, CPOs that blend into the environment would be utilized far more than bouncer-type protectors would. However, in certain situations the use of bouncer-type protectors would definitely have certain advantages. The use of female CPOs is also important, as in many situations, the Principal may be female. If a female CPO was not part of the protection detail, it would be difficult to provide effective protection. All in all, the specific operational situation would influence and determine what attributes a CPO for that specific operation should possess.

Desirable physical attributes

The physical attributes necessary for a CPO refer to the natural responses and physical capabilities that a CPO should possess. Many of these attributes can and should be developed through effective ongoing training. However, if a potential CPO does not have the natural tendencies or inherent physical attributes, it would then probably be fair to say that this person would probably not be a very proficient CPO.

The focus of physical attributes refers not only to the ability to deal physically with potential violent attacks but also with the physical stress and duress that may be placed on a CPO **during** operations. These may include the ability to handle long periods of inactivity interspersed with very intense periods of activity, coping for extended periods on little sleep and irregular eating patterns.

A female CPO may not have the necessary physical strength to deal with threats using strictly unarmed combat but would be invaluable to a protection team should they be protecting a female Principal. By having a female CPO on the team, the Principal could be accompanied into female toilets without attracting any undue attention.

In general, despite the disadvantage of not being as physically strong as men are, the use of alternative weaponry and comprehensive training would enable a female CPO to operate at the same level as her male counterparts. A common measure of physical capability is what is known as "drag or carry" competency. This involves a CPO having to carry or drag a dummy (between 50 kg and 75 kg) for approximately 25 meters, simulating the evacuation of a wounded Principal. If a CPO is competent to perform this activity, gender would not be a factor in determining operational competency.

Desirable Personality Characteristics

Personality-related characteristics can be described as those **psychological attributes** that dictate a person's ability to effectively manage both different people and situations. There are many aspects that could be identified and considered relevant under this heading. The following personality characteristics can be highlighted as being most relevant to close protection work:

+ patience
+ self-motivation
+ ability to operate alone or in a team
+ a positive mindset
+ a sense of humor.

Each of these factors is an inherent aspect of a person's psychological make up. Even if some of these factors are not prevalent, they can be developed through training and experience.

The author and Lourens Jacobs relax while on operation in West Africa.
(Note the quick-draw leg holster, which clearly illustrates
that this is an overt protection operation.)

However, if there is not a strong natural leaning towards these aspects, a potential CPO would, in all likelihood not be able to manage the rigors of the job. This may result in more than just the CPO losing his/her job but may mean loss of life for the Principal and/or members of the protection team. As emphasized by one expert: "a CPO must be able to operate under stressful situations and cope with boredom while maintaining a positive attitude."

Self Test

Name 5 personality attributes

Learned Skills

Learned skills refer to the **profile characteristics that must be taught and developed through training**. It also includes aspects that everyone may possess but may need to be more highly developed for CPO duties.

People and communication skills

These refer, primarily, to the tools needed to communicate effectively in all close protection-related situations. This concept would include the application of correct protocol and etiquette. In many operational situations, the CPO would need to secure the cooperation of persons who, although not part of the protection detail, could contribute to the success of an operation. These skills can be developed through basic training, including role-play and scenario staging, as well as on-the-ground experience.

Observation and awareness

One of a CPO's primary tasks is the early identification of threats. This would enable him/her to then implement the necessary measures needed to **avoid** these threats. The concept of pro-activity and avoidance is partly reliant on a CPO having excellent observation and awareness skills. These skills can be developed by training CPOs in the necessary techniques and principles that apply. It would then be vitally important for the trainee CPO to practice and develop these skills in realistic situations.

Self Test

Why is observation and awareness critical for a CPO?

Quick thinking and adaptability

The ability of a CPO to be able to think laterally and problem solve under pressure is vital to the protection initiative. The capability to blend into different environments and operate under vastly different circumstances is part and parcel of a high-level CPO's regular operational life.

While this is an inherent personality characteristic, it can most definitely be developed through effective training. The training should focus on presenting task-related problems in a manner as close as possible to what happens in reality. This should occur with an instructor guiding the trainee CPO through the problem until the trainee develops confidence to handle these problems alone.

Hard skills

Hard skills encompass all the necessary physical skills that a CPO needs to develop in order to provide effective close protection. The key hard

Self Test

What are hard skills?

skill areas are unarmed combat, driving skills, firearm skills, protection-related skills (IADs) and first aid skills (these are explained in more detail earlier in the book). These skills should be developed through ongoing training.

General Perceptions

The realities of what occurs while providing close protection is something that is often not discussed. It seems as if the vast majority of persons involved would rather believe the "glamorous side" of the close protection industry instead of looking at the harsh realities of what actually happens.

In many cases information security was cited as a reason as to why close protection is misunderstood. It is obvious that in an industry where operational methodology is designed to keep people alive, it would be important that such methodology was not available for public access.

While maintaining a certain level of discretion when referring to the sensitive aspects of close protection provision is a valid issue, the persons and organizations involved in the industry should at the very least be able to differentiate between fact and fiction.

It has also been noted that in many cases the perceptions that people related to a close protection operation have, directly affect the way that a protection operation is performed. There are three sub-groups of persons that were identified whose perceptions were relevant to this topic namely: the general public, clients utilizing the services of CPOs and, lastly, other security providers. Each of these will be briefly discussed below.

Public perception

In general, the public perception of close protection can only be based on hearsay or "what is seen in the movies." This, for the most part, would be an unrealistic picture of what actually happens, focusing on those aspects that are most entertaining. It is not exciting to watch somebody sit in a car outside a client's house for five hours not knowing when he or she is to depart.

Even though the public perception is important, most experts believe it is not necessary or viable to attempt to educate the general public on the realities of close protection.

The following reasons have been identified as to why it is not necessary to educate the general public on the realities of close protection:

1. As a direct result of the information security that is a fundamental part of any close protection operation, much of what the CPO does and how it is done should not be made available to the general public.

2. In any event, the public in general would not be interested in the fundamental details, as for the most part they are unexciting and quite monotonous.

3. Almost all members of the general public would never have a need for personal protection therefore there would be no point in educating them (making them more aware).

4. In certain cases, the current public perception may actually aid in the smooth facilitation of a protection operation. This may be so, in that people might be more willing to help or cooperate if they believe that close protection operations are "like the movies" as this would make them feel important.

Client perception

The importance of clarifying the clients[7] perceptions about close protection should not be underestimated. If clients are not aware of what a CPO should be able to do, as well has how close protection should be provided, the effective provision of protection is difficult. It may result in the misuse of protection staff or the client utilizing under-qualified personnel who may charge less and undercut the qualified protection providers.

Further common themes that can be identified relating to client misconceptions include, but are not limited to, some of the following:

- The belief that any ex-policeman or service person is qualified to work as a close protection operative even if they have never received formal CPO training
- That close protection duties include those of acting as a butler or servant to the client
- The concept that CPOs do not need ongoing training and retraining
- The idea that it does not really matter what qualifications a trained CPO possesses since it is better to have a less-competent person who perhaps is less expensive, than to have nobody at all.

It is clear that unless there is some sort of client education process that deals with some of the concerns mentioned above, effective regulation

---

[7] For the difference between the Principal and the client see *Appendix: Definitions*

will be difficult or impossible to achieve. The lack of client education may result in clients either paying too much for unqualified personnel and/or competing providers may actually engage in price wars in order to secure business. This could have disastrous results with either under-qualified personnel being employed or the operative on the ground not getting the correct remuneration for his/her services.

The fact that in many situations the client is actually not the Principal often has a direct influence on the quality of protection that the Princi-pal receives. In many cases, the clients requesting the services do not have the correct understanding of what comprehensive protection du-ties entail. As a direct result of this, on many occasions, clients will select service providers purely on price-related factors. This, in certain cases, has led to unqualified service providers being awarded contracts for the provision of close protection services.

CPO deployed on a protection detail.
(Note the dress of the CPO enables concealment of weaponry while still blending into the environment.)

Perceptions by General Security Companies
(such as guarding, alarm monitoring and installation, and investigation companies)

Within the security industry itself, it seems that close protection is a misunderstood and misrepresented specialization. This is mentioned as a point of relevance because in many cases, other security companies are requested to provide close protection services by their clients and may not utilize qualified and specialized CPO personnel during protection operations. Further, CPOs must liaise and work with providers of other security and related services.

The benefits of educating other security suppliers includes establishing the protection market for providers that only utilize trained personnel and that the client will probably receive a more effective close protection service. A general education package that outlines to security providers what the benefits of close protection are and what a qualified CPO's job description should be would be very useful. This is an answer to the problem of how to educate other security providers on close protection.

Moreover, this makes the working relationship between CPOs and other security providers far more efficient. This is relevant since, although a CPO is not a specialist in all fields of security, he/she should have a generic understanding of almost all aspects relevant to the security of the Principal. This means that a CPO would know what the functions of other security providers entail but in most cases, other security providers do not know enough about close protection to understand clearly, how it works.

Conclusion – Summary of Key Points

+   Identify and explain the relevant misconceptions related to close protection.
+   Outline the correct profile of a CPO in terms of physical, psychological, and learned skills was also discussed.
+   Three critical subgroups were identified when the topic of perception was mentioned, namely;
    1.   the public,
    2.   the clients who use close protection, and
    3.   other providers of security and related services.

Some of the key concepts that were mentioned with regard to the close protection operatives' profile are aspects such as his/her physical appearance and the relevant and personality characteristics that are needed to be an effective operative. The consensus was that a CPO should have the ability to look like the "average person on the street" in order to facilitate low-profile protection. This was outlined as far more important than the physical size of the CPO.

Some of the key psychological attributes that are mentioned included attributes such as patience, self-motivation, ability to operate alone or in a team, a positive mindset, and a good sense of humor.

An educating process (awareness program) for clients and other security providers is beneficial.

CHAPTER 6

Terrorism, the International Environment, and Close Protection

"Since the September 11 attacks people all over the world look at security differently, the importance of specialized security and Close Protection as a vital component to effective protection cannot be overestimated."
—Norman Steynberg

Introduction

One of the primary identified methods of reducing the likelihood of a direct terrorist attack on a designated person or of being an unwitting victim of such an attack, would be to utilize the services of trained CPOs. Not only will the presence of security **act as a deterrent** in itself, but it will also **minimize the risk of exposure** through applied avoidance and proactive planning.

The concept of a global world economy has influenced international trends in many ways. **One of these is the way in which terrorism could be perpetrated against targets on foreign soil and still achieves the desired effect on the terrorist's targeted audience.** Terrorist activity and attack on innocent civilians, in an attempt to achieve a desired political or religious outcome, is not a new threat to world security and safety.

Terrorist groups such as the Baader-Meinhof gang in Germany, the Red Army Faction in Japan (RAF), the Provisional Irish Republican Army (PIRA) in the United Kingdom as well as the Palestinian Liberation Organization (PLO) and Al-Fatah in Israel, to name but a few, have long been carrying out acts of terror. This has led to each country tackling terrorism in its own way.

Examples of this are the establishment of counter-terrorist teams (the British SAS, the Yamam in Israel, Delta Force in the United States, etc.) or taking such counter-terrorist action such as Israel placing undercover air marshals on all El-Al flights and proposals to arm pilots on American flights. However, the events of September 11, 2001, London, and Bali bombings have forever changed the public perception and international awareness of the terrorist threat.

Self Test
_____

Name 6 types of attacks terrorists use

Generally, terrorist attacks take one of the following forms:

+   hostage taking
+   hijacking
+   assassination
+   armed attack
+   bomb attack
+   propaganda and intimidation campaigns.

The fact that in the vast majority of cases the targets of terrorist attacks are non-combatants/civilians (see definition below) means that anybody could be a potential victims of a terrorist attack. With this concern in mind, the governments of most security-conscious nations have put considerable time and effort into the concepts of anti- and counter-terrorism. The need to deal with the terrorist phenomenon is understood by most security specialists and it is commonplace for security assessments to include an analysis of the likelihood of terrorist attack on a given target or person. In terms of proactive avoidance and prevention, the use of trained CPOs becomes a viable addition to any anti-terror campaign (particularly when specific individuals are vulnerable).

Key Principles
_____

1. **Random nature of attacks**
2. **High profile or influential persons**
3. **Desire is exposure and publicity for their given cause**

The most intimidating aspect of terrorism is the perceived "random nature" of attacks, particularly those aimed at spreading fear among the general population. However, there are those kinds of terrorist attacks where specific individuals are the target (for whatever reason). This is most relevant for a Principal requiring the services of a close protection detail.

More often than not clients utilizing close protection services are high-profile or influential persons. This means that if such persons were targeted by terrorist groups the potential media exposure (of the terrorist attack) and ramifications of such action would be greater, i.e., the terrorist group involved would get better exposure of its views and aims, particularly if politically motivated. From a terrorist perspective this is often exactly what they are looking for as in many cases what they desire is exposure and publicity for their given cause.

Definitions

There are many different definitions of terrorism. The breadth and scope of what is considered terrorism and what is not is constantly being changed and adjusted. When reviewing terrorism as a specialist field it is staggering to see the subdivisions of terrorism. There are many specialist subcategories ranging from aspects such as bio-terrorism to complex issues like state terrorism. For the purpose of this book the definitions of terrorism contained in Title 22 of the United States Codes, Section 2656 (d) will be used. The term is the best defined therein and reads as follows: [8]

> *The term 'terrorism' means premeditated, politically motivated violence perpetrated against non-combatant targets by sub national groups or clandestine agents, usually intended to influence an audience.*
>
> *The term 'international terrorism' means terrorism involving citizens or the territory of more than one country.*
>
> *The term 'terrorist group' means any group practicing or that has significant subgroups that practice international terrorism*

What differentiates a terrorist attack from a criminal offense?
In many cases, a terrorist attack would involve criminal offenses, e.g., murder, assault, etc. This is not, however, true for the converse. According to the above definition, for an act to be considered an act of terror the following key aspects need to be apparent:[9]

- It needs to be a premeditated act, in other words it must have been planned in advance. No terrorist act is a spur of the moment act. While the victims and location may not have been preselected, the act itself would have involved a certain amount of planning. The motivation for the attack could be based on political, cultural, religious, or social beliefs.

---

[8]   It should be noted that there are many existing definitions of terrorism and terrorist activities, this definition has been chosen merely because it is a well-referenced example. The selection of this definition by no means validates its accuracy above that of other definitions.

[9]   The information below has been extracted and compiled from: *Terrorism inside a world phenomenon* (Davies,: 14-15); and *Inside Terrorism* (Hoffman,: 13-43).

- The attack or act is usually an act of violence perpetrated against non-combatants. For purposes of the above definition, the term non-combatant is interpreted to include, in addition to civilians, military personnel who at the time of the incident are unarmed and/or not on duty. Civilian security personnel, such as Executive Protection Personnel, unless openly armed, are also seen as non-combatants.

Self Test

- What makes a terrorist attack different from a criminal act?
- What do they have in common?

- The last key aspect relevant to defining a terrorist act is usually the attempt to gain exposure for the terrorist group's cause by means of the ensuing media coverage of the terrorist action. In his book, *Inside Terrorism*, Hoffman devotes an entire chapter to this issue. Some of the key points that are mentioned by Hoffman are as follows:

  - The fact that many terrorist acts are planned in such a manner as to get maximum press and media coverage.

  - The concept that many people will be informed about who the terrorist group perpetrating the act are and why the group did it, is sometimes motivation for terrorist action in itself.

  - The constant battle of television networks and other media forms to gain ratings and increase circulation means that the more extravagant the terrorist act the more media exposure each will get.

Therefore, a terrorist attack by definition will usually include some sort of criminal offense (murder, attempted murder, arson, assault, etc.), whereas a criminal attack may not demonstrate any of the factors that define a terrorist action. It is often the intention behind the action that will determine whether it is an act of terror or simply a criminal act.

Scene from a recent political rally held in London.

Terrorism and Close Protection

By definition, almost all close protection activities attempt to **minimize the Principal's exposure to every relevant threat.** The Principals' exposure would be primarily dependant on his or her profile in terms of aspects such as public appearances or political activity. If the Principal is a high-profile figure (featured regularly in the media; well known, i.e., a celebrity; or holds a position of influence, for instance in business, politics, or entertainment) any of

> **Key Principle**
> _____
> Minimize the Principal's exposure to every relevant threat

the aspects listed below can increase the likelihood of terrorist groups targeting him/her:

+   his/her political beliefs
+   his/her religious beliefs
+   his/her nationality
+   his/her business dealings
+   his/her personal likes and dislikes
+   the people that the Principal socializes with or is affiliated with.

The more the CPO knows about the above-mentioned factors the easier it will be to determine what level of exposure the Principal may have to a terrorist attack. This would then enable the CPO to plan and implement such strategies to minimize the likelihood of attack occurring. Contingencies must also be developed to cover all relevant aspects in terms of how to deal with attacks if they were to occur.

Finally, in terms of a terrorist attack, the last aspect to consider is **"wrong place, wrong time."** This means that simply by being at a certain geographical location at the wrong moment in time, the Principal may be exposed to acts of terror. Nonetheless, even this random, unforeseen exposure can be minimized. A CPO must minimize the chances of "wrong place, wrong time" by being up to date with terrorist groups' modus operandi and planning the Principal's movements in such a way as to limit the time the Principal will be in such situations or locations.

> **Key Principle**
> _____
> Your client could be a victim simply by being at the wrong place, at the wrong time

Random acts of terror are exceptionally difficult to predict and avoid. However, effective prediction and avoidance could be achieved by employing close protection operatives and risk management professionals. Terrorism is considered a "must learn" topic for all professional CPOs. A professional CPO must have a basic knowledge of terrorist groups and modus operandi. This is important as otherwise it is impossible to carry out a comprehensive risk and threat analysis, resulting in the limited effectiveness of planning and contingency planning.

Avoidance of any threatening situation could be considered the primary goal of close protection. A well-trained CPO tasked with the protection of a Principal who could potentially be a victim of terrorist attack should consider it a primary aspect of his/her duties to liaise regularly with relevant authorities as well as conduct ongoing research and fieldwork so as to be able to constantly plan and adapt according to the identified changing trends.

Self Test

Name 7 reasons why people are targeted

In their book, *You're the Target: Coping with Terror and Crime*, Shackley, Oatman, and Finney outline their belief that effective close protection in certain cases could be considered enough of a deterrent for would be assassins, stalkers, and terrorist attackers to select easier or less protected victims.

International Environment and Terrorism

The significance of the 9/11 act of terrorism in the United States as well as the London and Bali bombings has been extensive. It was not only the number of people who died in these particular incidents, (especially the 9/11 attack) that had such far-reaching after effects (such as the United States actions against Afghanistan and Iraq). If a comparison is drawn between this specific act (9/11) and other continuous terrorist activity there have, in fact, been many more civilians killed over a period of time in places like Latin America, the Middle East and certain Pacific-based countries than in 9/11. The resulting widespread fear and insecurity in American citizens post-9/11 could perhaps be linked to the widespread media exposure at the time of the 9/11 attack and the fact that the attacks were conducted on such a large scale, for the first time on American soil and that America appeared defenseless against the onslaught. American public fears and insecurities have subsequently been compounded by the ongoing media focus and attention given to the "global war against terrorism."

It could be said that the 9/11 attack made people all over the world reassess their security, personal and otherwise. Furthermore, people may have also started to analyze what they could possibly do to enhance their safety when traveling abroad. A practical example of this is the huge drop in air travel by tourists for a while after 9/11. One of the obvious answers for those who could afford it was to employ the services of security specialists (CPOs).

It is a widely known fact in security circles that something often referred to as the "international terrorist network" is in operation and was at its prime in the 1980s and 1990s. This network had been established, where terrorists from unrelated groups received training and established informal networks. In certain cases, this included cooperation in planning operations and drawing support from each other.

This means that knowledge and information was shared across borders. The implication of this network is that there could well be a continuous threat to certain high-profile individuals regardless of where a VIP might be traveling in the world. An

Key Points

- International terrorist network
- A CPO needs to stay up to date and congruent with all threats

example of this is the attack at Ben Gurion airport in the late 1970s by members of a terrorist group known as the Red Army Faction. This attack was apparently perpetrated on behalf of Middle Eastern terrorists and carried out by German and Japanese terrorists.

Therefore, with both **the internationalization of the media and international operations of terrorist groups being well established**, it is easy to recognize that terrorists could achieve their objectives by selecting targets that may be far removed from their home country. So too with business, now being run on a global scale and international deals becoming the mainstay of large business operations, a VIP business executive may travel abroad often. *It would therefore be vital for a CPO to be up-to-date and congruent with all threats in any specific set travel destination including potential terrorist or related activity.*

The Al-Qaeda[10] terrorist network is said to be active in over 60 countries. Furthermore, their modus operandi is so varied that some governments are devoting entire units to try and track down traces of the network in their own countries. For individuals without such resources, employing CPOs that can liaise with such units and work to minimize the associated risks to the Principal would be a practical measure to employ. Without effective specialist security professionals conducting ongoing liaison and research it would be almost impossible to determine when, where, why, and how an attack may take place.

---

[10] The Al-Qaeda terrorist network is considered one the world's foremost terrorist organizations, it is estimated to be active in over 60 countries and is alleged to be responsible for the 9/11 attacks and the Bali bombings in Indonesia. Its leader Osama Bin Ladin is one of the world's most wanted terror suspects.

Fundamentalist Attacks

> *We issue the following Fatwa to all Muslims: The ruling to kill the Americans and their allies...civilians and military...is an individual duty for every Muslim who can do it in any country in which it is possible to do it...*
> (Quote from a video taped interview with Osama Bin Laden on October 7, 2001).[11]

In security and safety terms, the concept of fundamentalist attacks is a very disturbing idea. The fact that a person would be willing to trade their life in order to achieve a given objective is in itself a worrying concept for any security personnel. When that objective possibly involves perpetrating violent acts on a CPO's Principal, it is vital for CPOs to not only be aware of fundamentalist behavior, but also how to manage and deal with it. This is obviously no small task but modern methods of terrorists necessitate the need for counter skills to fundamentalist attack.

The willingness of fundamentalists to sacrifice themselves makes them a very difficult threat to manage.

Fundamentalism is not a new concept. However, it takes on a different perspective when assessing its impact on close protection and close protection strategies (the need to protect a designated person from any threatening situation). An attack by a fundamentalist terrorist is a major problem since regardless of the form of attack (suicide bombing, fire arms attack, etc.) **if an individual is willing to lay down his or her life in order to achieve the objective, he or she will make a very difficult adversary to defend against and protect a Principal's life.**

Self Test

Name 3 misconceptions about terrorists

There are many misconceptions about fundamentalist attackers. Information on the profile of fundamentalist terrorists is mentioned in the publications of Lacquer (79–105) and Hoffman (157–185). Some of the predomi-

---

[11] The excerpt was extracted from material utilized by Mr. C. McGuire (see references for details on Mr. McGuire) in a lecture on terrorism to Japanese embassy staff, presented in Johannesburg on the November 12, 2001. The original quote was taken from a CNN news update that screened the above-mentioned video interview.

nant misconceptions are that terrorists are uneducated, badly trained, and easy to spot.

However, from the vast majority of case studies that are available, these aspects seem to be untrue. This may mean that the fundamentalist attacker may be a well-educated, highly motivated attacker and even a professional soldier who will be able to preempt and avoid many security and close protection initiatives, plans, or measures.

It is vital that a CPO's training and operational practices prepare him/her with the skills and knowledge of how to avoid, manage, or deal with a terrorist attack should it occur. In order to achieve this, all aspects of a CPO's training need to be integrated into a focused protective strategy. When analyzing the applicable factors needed in order for close protection operatives to deal with this sort of threat, the following aspects have been identified:

1. Effective risk and threat assessment skills should be included in all close protection training in order to be aware of the latest modus operandi of current fundamentalist terrorist groups. This would also give the CPO the ability to identify any threats that are inherent as a result of geographical location and Principal characteristics/ lifestyle.

2. A CPO should utilize effective planning skills in order to preempt all potential attacks and threatening situations. The aim is to avoid such situations and to plan for identified contingencies that may arise should a situation occur.

3. Effective delegation, manpower, and logistical appreciation and application of skills are vital in order to correctly forecast and then deploy the necessary close protection structures. This is done in order to create layers of defense around the Principal and limit his/her exposure to identified threats.

4. Effective awareness and observational skills training should be a core part of close protection training in order to enable CPOs to identify the subtle indicators that may precede an attack situation.

5. Mental acuity and lateral thinking ability should be part of a CPO's characteristics. This should enable a CPO to be prepared for different contingencies and many unexpected situations that may occur.

6. Effective immediate action drill (IAD) reflex training should be a mainstay of close protection team training. This would assist in ensuring that under the pressure of an attack situation the close protection detail will respond in the correct fashion.

While a fundamentalist terrorist attack is a most daunting reality, effective training covering the factors discussed above should prepare the CPO to deal with and manage most attacks should they actually occur.

Effects of International and Local Terrorism on Close Protection

Critical factors were identified that influence the way terrorism affects Close Protection. These aspects pertain to both local and international trends. These factors will be outlined and discussed below:

Key Points

1. Foreign travel of VIP's can add to threat levels
2. International terrorist networks give potential attackers greater reach
3. Terrorists use the media as a tool
4. Your Principal's profile may make them a target

1. Foreign travel of VIPs

Almost all people that warrant the services of a CPO or CPO team will travel abroad relatively often. Even if the CPO or team does not accompany the VIP it falls within the scope and duties of the CPO to conduct a thorough risk and threat assessment of the situation at the intended destination of travel. The CPO must then brief the Principal accordingly.

It is therefore vital that a CPO is up-to-date with international trends and occurrences. Furthermore, the CPO must have the ability to access the correct logistical and situational threat related information as well as make contact with key personnel on the ground at the Principal's intended destination. This is important since the threat of terrorist attack may vary from country to country and region to region.

2. International terrorist networks

The fact that most established terrorist groups have contact with each other and assist each other where possible poses a unique problem to the CPO. The problem is that due to a Principal's status, nationality, religious persuasions, and/or political beliefs there may be a risk from foreign groups targeting him or her in countries where such a group is not believed to be active.

3. Media leveraging

Many VIPs utilizing close protection services can be classified as high-profile (easily recognizable by the public and regularly featured in the media). This means that a terrorist organization wanting media exposure for their cause would attract a lot of attention by perpetrating an attack (murder, kidnap, destruction of assets, embarrassment, etc.) on a high profile VIP. It is well documented that media coverage and exposure to a larger audience base is a common motive for terrorist attacks.

4. Principal's background, religious, and/or political beliefs and affiliations

A Principal may be targeted solely because of his/her background, religious, and/or political beliefs and affiliations. The reasons for this, in addition to possible media coverage, may be strictly personal as fanatical followers belonging to a fundamentalist terrorist group may take personal offence to a public figure who extols different beliefs and ideals to them (for example, the Fatwa pronounced on the author Salman Rushdie for his novels on aspects of the Muslim religion, which upset certain sections of this religion's adherents).

Self Test

Name 4 aspects of the Principals profile that may make them a possible target

Ramifications of Terrorist Activities for the Training of Close Protection Operatives

Knowledge of terrorist training, methodology, and activities, should form part of any close protection training program. It is important for a CPO to know how his opposition trains, prepares and executes its actions. Within the context of international terrorism and fundamentalist attacks (i.e., the usually suicidal nature of these attacks and the attacker's absolute disdain for their own lives in accomplishing an attack on their selected target) the key question to be clarified is:

How does terrorism and its modern applications impact
on the required training and operational practices of
close protection operatives?

To answer this question, a comprehensive and holistic approach needs to be adopted for the training of CPOs. This is not specifically because of the increase in the threat level of terrorist attacks, but also because the worldwide proliferation of terrorist activities remains a major contributing factor to the need for highly trained CPOs.

Terrorism is not a new threat but the combination of modern technology and improved weaponry as well as the easy access to information (Internet) has made the potential for terrorist attacks an even greater concern. When assessing additions or adjustments needed for CPO training the following areas appear to be most relevant:

- The CPO's ability to use of technology (Internet) to gain information as fast and accurately as possible.
- The CPO's ability to effectively conduct a complete, accurate threat assessment and risk analysis.
- Effective liaison skills is a must-have attribute for CPOs in order to stay as informed as possible by gaining relevant information from authorities.

- ❖ A combination of the abilities needed to plan thoroughly, while also being able to adjust and adapt based on the sudden changes in a given situation.
- ❖ The CPO must also obviously maintain adequate competency levels of all the relevant hard skills (unarmed combat, firearms skills, etc.) as relevant to the function of Close Protection.

Conclusion – Summary of Key Points

While acts of terror are not a new threat to the safety of civilians, recent acts of terror such as the 9/11 attacks, London and the Bali bombings have changed the relevance of the threat to many people. In terms of close protection activities it is vital for CPOs to know what the existing threats to their Principal may be, as well as when, where and how these threats may manifest.

The link between the effective application of close protection and minimizing the levels of exposure to potential terrorist activity are well noted. However, factors such as the fact that many Principals are high-profile figures who may travel internationally often mean that a CPO needs to stay abreast of changing terrorist modus operandi trends and threats. This needs to be done in order for the CPO to minimize the Principal's exposure to such threats. There is existing proof that international terrorist organizations have widespread networks operating in many countries.

In order to minimize the risks of terror attacks, there are certain aspects of close protection training that need to be emphasized. These include aspects such as comprehensive networking and information gathering skills that would be needed to gain information on terrorist activities from the relevant agencies and official organizations. This would then enable the CPO to plan effectively in order to limit the exposure of a Principal to identified threats. Effective planning would also enable the CPO to consider contingencies and make the necessary preparations to manage such contingencies should they occur. It would also obviously be vital for a CPO to be competent in all necessary hard skills (firearms, unarmed combat, etc.) should an attack actually occur.

Close protection operatives need to have, at the very least, a good understanding of terrorism, including motivation and general modus operandi of terrorist attackers. This is validated by the need for a CPO to be able to provide a comprehensive service, which must focus on the relevant threats facing a Principal or Principals.

CHAPTER 7

TECHNOLOGY, COMMUNICATION, AND CLOSE PROTECTION

"The ability for a CPO to effectively liaise and communicate with all parties involved in a Close Protection task is one of the most important attributes. It is a fundamental skill necessary to do the job in a professional manner."
—David M. Sharp

Introduction

In its most basic definition, Close Protection involves the safeguarding of a designated person's life. With such high stakes involved, it is obvious that any miscommunication could have very serious consequences. A vital operational skills requirement for a CPO is for the CPO to be able to effectively communicate and liaise with all relevant parties.

While the topic of communication is mentioned in many other Close Protection manuals, it is noted that a detailed working analysis of the communication aspects of close protection is often not covered in much detail. The clarification of this subject in the context of Close Protection will be expanded on in this chapter. The aim of this chapter is not to serve as an instructional framework but rather as a **detailed breakdown for the application of communication and related concepts during close protection operations.**

Furthermore, it can be mentioned that a thorough understanding of the aspects covered in this chapter should not only be well known to all close protection trainers but to field operatives as well. A further theme that is of importance is the applying of technological improvements to all aspects of close protection operations and training. This concept goes hand-in-hand with communication as improved technology enables a more effective means for CPOs to gather information and communicate.

Technological improvements have not only enabled more effective communication but have had effects on almost all close protection equipment, ranging from better firearms to GPS tracking systems. Several of these modifications and new operational equipment will be discussed later in this chapter. It should also be noted that while improvements in technology have huge benefits for the close protection industry, there is the reality that potential attackers could utilize these tools as well. This would obviously make it far more difficult to provide comprehensive protection for a high-risk Principal.

Key Principle

The reality that potential attackers use these improved technological tools as well

Communication in Close Protection

There is much information available on the principles that are applicable to general communication. Some of these principles will be briefly outlined below and then will be applied to Close Protection. As outlined in the Behavior Systems Development's *Train-the-Trainer Manual*, effective communication should follow the sequence below:

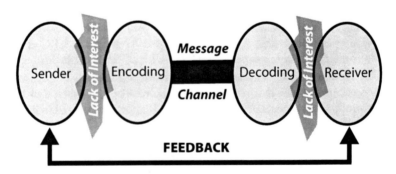

Diagram 1: Process of Communication.
(Behavior Systems Development A: 71)

Regardless of the medium for communication, CPOs should utilize the key steps as outlined in the above diagram. These aspects, which are applicable to communication in all situations, should be implemented by **CPOs to avoid miscommunication.** An example relating to the above diagram to a close protection situation could be a Principal briefing (see, Appendix: Definitions). If the close protection team leader (sender)

Key Principles

1. Avoid miscommunication
2. Resulting consequences could be severe
3. Whatever the reason for not effectively communicating, the consequences could cost lives

does not effectively put the information across in an understandable format (encoding and sending) and if the Principal (receiver) does not understand (decode) and confirm (provide feedback) that he/she understands what is required the resulting consequences could be severe.

If we were to take the above example and assume that the protection team leader would be briefing a Principal on the "do's and don'ts" of reacting to a hand grenade attack and if the message, for whatever reason is not effectively communicated the consequences could cost lives of the Principal and protection team. This is simply one example but the concepts could be applied to almost all aspects of close protection.

Avoiding a Breakdown of Communication in Close Protection

The topic of communication as applied to Close Protection is very broad; therefore, it is necessary to subdivide it into more easily explained subcategories. When referring to communication as related specifically to Close Protection, we are able to subdivide it into the following categories:

*   Communication between team members of a close protection detail
*   Communication between team members of a close protection detail and the Principal or client
*   Communication between CPOs and relevant persons in the external environment.

The importance of each of these areas cannot be understated. They are each vital components that are essential for a close protection operation to not only be successful but also efficient.

Communication Between Close Protection Team Members

The subdivision of internal communications within a close protection team can be broken down into two subsections; namely, everyday communication and communication under attack. These will be discussed below.

Everyday Communication

In order to understand "everyday communication" within a close protection team this aspect needs to be further subdivided. It can be broken down into three primary subdivisions; namely, communication before an operation, communication during the operation, and, lastly, communication after an operation.

Self Test
___

Name 3 types of communication relevant to close protection

Communication aspects before a close protection operation

In terms of verbal and written communication, pre-operation communication would include an operation's warning, comprehensive advance work, and planning; an operations order; and a full face-to-face team briefing. This process would usually first involve telephonic communication and then face-to-face verbal communication in order to pass on all relevant information.

Communication aspects during a close protection operation
Communication during a close protection operations would be either through hand radios, cellular phones, and/or face-to-face verbal com-

munication. In addition, certain close protection operatives advocate the use of hand signals to communicate concepts during an operation.

The identified benefits of using hand signals are as follows:

The author (back to camera) briefing a CPO detail during an operation.

- ⋆ it is simple and quick to communicate short messages
- ⋆ it provides minimal interruption for the Principal
- ⋆ it enhances team work through the implementation of forced visual contact at regular intervals between team members.

Communication aspects after a close protection operation
This phase of an operation would usually involve a debriefing for all team members as well as the application of feedback systems either written or verbal. Communication after an operation is often not given the

necessary attention in close protection manuals but is vitally important. *If CPOs and other relevant parties involved in a close protection operation are not able to learn from mistakes that may have been made during the operation, it would be difficult to ensure that the same mistakes do not happen again.*

Key Principle

Learn from mistakes made during the operation and ensure they do not happen again

Communication during an attack

While the primary objective of close protection may be centered on the avoidance of any potentially dangerous situation, the reality of violent attack is most definitely something which a CPO should be trained to handle. The research for this book indicated that there is a concern as to how many CPOs who were trained in the past, but have had no retraining, would respond when actually faced with a life-threatening situation. A major reason why CPO teams may not react effectively could be because of inefficient communication while under the stress of an attack.

The key aspect of how communication takes place during an attack on the Principal (AOP) is that communication during an attack should be trained to be an instinctive response. It should be a fundamental aspect of the IAD training that forms the basis for CPO response to threatening situations.

A CPO detail practicing IADs .
(Note the level of cover they are providing for the VIP.)

While there are several definitions of IAD's, the definition selected for this book is taken from the Dynamic Alternatives' *Close Protection Training Manual:* "These are planned, trained responses to an attack or threatening situation in any given environment" (Dynamic Alternatives: 34). The levels of communication that should take place during an IAD are illustrated in the flow chart on the following page:

Step 1

A CPO identifies an attack and should then, if possible, communicate the following key pieces of information to the rest of his/her team members:

Self Test

Name 3 actions to be taken during an attack

- Direction of attack (clock or directional method, see Appendix: Definitions)
- Form or type of attack
- Description of the attacker/ attackers
- Respond that he/she will engage the attacker/s

Step 2

(It should be noted that the aspects below should all happen simultaneously)

- The CPO identifying the attack should, if it is possible to do so, communicate a warning to the attacker (e.g., "drop the gun")
- The designated bodyguard should tell the Principal what is happening, e.g., "Your life is being threatened please stay behind me," and based on pre-rehearsed reaction the bodyguard will simultaneously provide body cover and evacuate the Principal
- The rest of the team members will either provide back-up for the CPO who is engaging the attacker, and/or assist in providing additional bodycover for the bodyguard and Principal as they evacuate

Step 3

- A detailed evaluation and assessment of the situation after evacuation should be done by the team leader. The team leader would then make a decision on what should happen next.

Flow Chart 1: Communication during IADs (immediate action drills).

The steps outlined at left are **simply a generic example,** but the format could be applied to most attack-related IADs that a close protection team would need.

Why It is Difficult to Communicate Effectively During Attacks and IADs

Probably the key reason making it difficult to communicate under attack is as a direct result of the "flight or fight" survival instincts. Under the extreme duress of an attack a CPO's survival instincts will trigger a huge amount of adrenal release, known as adrenal dump. There are many signs and symptoms of adrenal dump that effect a CPO's reactions, not all of these are helpful to a CPO while executing an IAD.

Geoff Thompson, in his book *Dead or Alive,* describes many of the symptoms that are triggered during adrenal release. The adrenal release symptoms that effect communication are as follows:

1. Freeze or panic – If a CPO is not trained to make the correct reflexive reactions, he/she may freeze or panic under the stress of a real attack. In order to avoid freezing or panicking, skills need to be developed in a manner that is as close to what will occur in reality as possible (Thompson: 85–101).

2. Auditory exclusion or distortion – This makes it difficult to hear clearly or distorts that which is actually heard.

3. Verbal inability – A circumstance characterized by an inability to communicate complex material verbally. This occurs as a direct result of the part of the brain that runs the formation of complex speech patterns shutting down as a direct result of adrenaline causing flight-or-fight instinct.

4. Memory distortion – This basically refers to the fact that under extreme duress a person will only respond reflexively (apply innate survival instincts). Therefore, for an IAD reaction to be effective it needs to be practiced repetitively until it becomes reflexive.

5. Flinch response – Another barrier to effective communication under attack is known as the "flinch response." The flinch response is the human body's instinctive reaction when faced with an occurrence that it was not prepared for. The flinch response involves three key actions namely:
   + A sharp inhalation
   + Physically moving away from the threat
   + Hands and arms being drawn into the chest or face area for protection.

The relevance of these three responses in terms of communication difficulties for a CPO under attack is focused on the first action of the flinch response, a sharp inhalation. This is a reflex action and can make regulated breathing difficult, which in turn would make verbal communication and clear thinking difficult for a CPO experiencing a flinch response.

How to Overcome the Identified Barriers to Communication

1. Realistic training and scenarios

Key Performance

- Scenario-based training is most effective to prepare for a life or death situation
- Short, clear communication with relevant information as quickly as possible is vital

"Realistic, repetitive scenario-based training is the most effective way to ensure that a CPO functions effectively in a life-or-death situation."
—Clinton McGuire

The statement above refers to the fact that repetitive rehearsal and practice under realistic conditions assists in acclimatizing CPOs to attack situations. This should enable them to function and communicate more effectively under the pressure of an actual attack on Principal situation.

2. Use of key words to shorten and simplify communication

The use of shortened key words to represent more complex concepts enables more knowledge to be communicated and understood. This could be achieved by applying aspects such as: implementing a directional approach as opposed to a clock system approach (see Appendix: Definitions).

Key Principles
------
1. Encounter threat
2. Counter threat
3. Evacuate Principal

Through repetitive practice during training, protection team members develop trust and an intimate understanding of procedures that should be followed under attack. This generally means that if an attack was to take place within a CPO's given area of responsibility (see Appendix: Definitions) then he/she would verbally communicate it to the rest of the team.

"Communication under attack should be short, clear, direct and pass on as much relevant information as quickly as possible."
—Johan Van Eck

The communication from the CPO who identified the attack to the rest of the team would be based on a key identifying aspect such as the color of the attacker's shirt or one of the attacker's prominent physical characteristics. These would assist the other team members in quickly identifying the attacker. The weapon or method of attack should also be communicated in as succinct a manner as possible, e.g., gun or knife attack. To illustrate that he/she was unhurt and capable of engaging the attacker, a CPO might use the word "mine" or "engaging" to inform the rest of the team members and let them know that he/she is dealing with the attack. A fellow team member could then utilize words like "cover" or "back-up" to let the rest of the team know that he/she is assisting the CPO who is engaging the attack.

Self Test

What must the CPO identify and communicate during an attack?

At this stage, the rest of the team would then concentrate on the evacuation of the Principal while taking into account the potential for secondary attacks or ambushes. The CPO or CPOs dealing with the attack would evacuate when the attackers were neutralized or the Principal was removed from the threat.

Communication Between Team Members and the Principal

The amount of direct communication between the protection team and the Principal would vary based on the following aspects: (S.P.W.T.)

+ the **size** of the close protection team
+ the relevant **protocol** based on the Principal's status or office
+ the Principal's **wishes**
+ the identified **threat** level

The Principal may or may not communicate directly with regular close protection team members. The Principal may chose to talk only to the bodyguard or team leader. It would then be the responsibility of the bodyguard or team leader to communicate with the rest of the team. It is also commonplace for the majority of communication to take place via the Principal's personal assistant or if an official, via the aid-de-camp.

Self Test

Name 4 aspects that affect the amount of direct communication between team members and the Principal

While taking these various differences in channels of communication into consideration there should, at the very least, be a Principal briefing (see Appendix: Definitions) and regular security update sessions.

Probably the key factors influencing the frequency and format of everyday communication would be the Principal's personality and the professionalism of the protection team. Sometimes the CPO's relationship becomes almost one of a good friend or close associate. This occurs as a direct result of the amount of time that the Principal and CPO spend together. If this is allowed to occur, the CPO's ability to operate professionally may be impaired. It is noted that a CPO should always maintain a professional emotional distance from his/her Principal.

Furthermore, another aspect to be considered is the communication between the team and the Principal under attack situations. Once again all the "difficulty factors" mentioned in the section on "team communication under attack" are applicable here. The concept should be to inform the Principal of what is going on and of the necessary actions that need to be taken in as short and simple a manner as possible. A common practice among CPOs is to only refer to the Principal by his/her surname and only address him/her formally, except when under attack. The change in form of address would act as an indicator to the Principal that the situation was serious.

It has also been found that the Principal may listen more effectively when this "first name" system is implemented in an emergency as opposed to if it is not. An example of the communication that might take place during an attack could be: *"John, we are being shot at. Get down and move to the cars."*

Communication Between CPOs and the External Environment (Liaison Skills)

> *"A CPO's ability to organize logistics and ensure the assistance of any external party who could make an operation run more smoothly is vital. This skill is probably the most common way a client will assess and measure the value for money of their Protectors."*
> —Jared Higgins

CPOs need to liaise with many different people to run an effective protection operation. This liaison could take on many forms and the **CPO needs to be an expert at interpersonal communication** while **maintaining operational security**. There is no way that a CPO can operate in an information or communication vacuum. In fact, one of the key reasons why former law enforcement personnel often excel as private sector CPOs is because of their established networks and connections, gained while employed by government agencies. Their knowledge of military or police aspects, such as their understanding of chain of command and the applicable protocols, become very valuable tools.

During a close protection operation one of the first external liaisons would take place while conducting advance work. Advance work can be defined as: "The process of gathering and sorting all necessary information in order to effectively plan and then actually run the specific operation." It is at this stage that communications may be necessary with some of the following external parties:

+ Police or related agencies
+ Hotels or other accommodation venues
+ Airlines and relevant handling agents
+ Venue organizers and staff
+ Security managers or other officials who may be engaged in an operation
+ Hospitals and medical centers
+ Any tourist officials who may provide assistance or advice
+ Any other party who may be able to contribute to the success of an operation.

While performing protective duties, the protection detail will constantly, as is necessary, liaise with civilians in the immediate environment. This is vital in order for the operation to run smoothly. Communicating with external parties may take many forms. An example could simply be liaising with the hotel concierge to organize extra rooms.

A more detailed external liaison may be liaising with the relevant police contact person in order to get a police escort for a protection motorcade.

> *"The key fundamental is that if the CPO cannot commu-nicate effectively and organize assistance from the relevant people, it would be almost impossible to run an efficient and secure close protection operation."*
> —Gavriel Schneider

Some additional communication-related aspects that are relevant when assessing how to train and prepare CPOs for operational duties are outlined below:

+ Teaching CPO trainees liaison protocols and communication skills is vital in close protection but they are very seldom covered in enough detail during CPO training courses. When these skills are taught the focus seems to be on a superficial overview with very little assessment or evaluations being conducted. It is important that a prospective CPO can communicate effectively and efficiently. The ability to convince relevant external parties to assist or provide information on a close protection operation becomes necessary for civilian CPOs. This is primarily because they operate without government backing and authority and therefore cannot instruct people to assist them.
+ In addition CPOs need to be trained in the correct procedure to follow in order to secure relevant:

1. information,
2. assistance, and
3. cooperation from both official and unofficial external parties.

This is important, since if a CPO ends up offending any persons who are involved, it can make the smooth running of an operation very difficult. This may even result in the Principal being under additional threat because of inefficient organization.

How Technology and Communications Affect CPOs

There have been technological improvements within the field of personal communication equipment utilized by CPOs. Not only have there been vast modifications with hand-held radios and hands-free voice activated microphones, but the wide distribution of cell phones and satellite phones have enabled easy international communication for protection details to be brought to a new level.

How technology is affecting the training of CPOs

The development of technological training aids and tools has, without a doubt, enhanced the way that CPOs are trained. The list of training aids is extensive and enables training to more closely mimic reality. One of the major benefits of some of this technology (use of video projectors and realistic firearm models) is that close protection trainees can practice dealing with potentially dangerous situations in a safe environment. This limits the exposure of trainees to unnecessarily dangerous risks while training them effectively.

The ease of use of modern paintball guns and Simunition (often referred to simply as Sim) bring a low level of risk to the student but adds to the reality of IAD training. The use of a multimedia approach to training is also becoming a core part of close protection training. Use of computer projectors, videos, and CDs in training has provided the trainer with a large variety of media and techniques that can be used to communicate information to students.

The Influence of the Internet on Close Protection

The Internet and the proliferation of the worldwide web have had an enormous influence over all sectors of trade and industry. This holds true for the close protection industry as well. The Internet has created **huge benefits**, as well as **additional threats and risks** for CPOs. Probably, the major benefits would revolve around the ease of access to information and the efficiency and speed of email communication. The associated risks stem from the ease of communication and access of information for attackers.

The proliferation of the Internet has several points that have to be taken into consideration since they have a direct effect on the close protection industry (these will be discussed below).

Ease of long-distance networking
The Internet has made both the benchmarking of standards and the creation of national/international networks relatively easy. These networks could assist in sharing relevant information. Having established contacts with direct email access makes the accessing of necessary operational information relatively easy and quick to **verify** or **query**.

Easy access to close protection operational methodology
This refers to the fact that any interested parties can download or access close protection training methodology and operational principles on the Internet. The negative impact of this is that it is now easy for potential attackers to find out how CPOs train, as well as how they would probably operate and react to different attack scenarios. This gives the potential attacker an opportunity to spot the weaknesses of a CPO team when planning an attack. This obviously poses a serious problem for CPOs.

On the positive side, this also provides CPOs located anywhere in the world the opportunity to obtain the most up-to-date methods and best practices. This is useful as it can be built into training as well as operational methodology.

Access to a Principal's personal and company information
"I found out things that I did not even know about my CEO [Principal] on the Internet…" was a statement made by one expert during the research for this book.

The impact of important confidential information being accessed via the Internet means that a potential attacker or merely someone out to discredit a Principal may be able to gain that information if he/she knows how to access it. Conversely, the same ease of access to information also makes the conducting of risk analysis and Principal Profiling easier for CPOs. This is especially relevant when planning international travel, where information on the current political situation in foreign countries needs to be obtained and assessed with planning foreign operations.

> **Self Test**
>
> - What are the pros and cons of the Internet?
> - How will you best use both to give you the advantage when protecting a Principal?

Technological Improvements on Close Protection Equipment and Tools

> *"While it is important for a CPO not to become depen-*
> *dant on tools and equipment, a professional CPO should*
> *carry a wide array of weaponry and related equipment."*
> —David M. Sharp

Tools and equipment utilized by CPOs is quite a broad topic. It can be broken down into subcategories and will make it easier for the reader to follow. These subdivisions are as follows and each will be discussed below: (W.T.A.)

+ **W**eaponry
+ **T**echnology
+ **A**ccessories

Technological improvements of close protection weaponry

The ongoing research and development by forward-thinking companies (such as Glock and ASP International), as well as the application of technological improvements in almost all the weaponry used by CPOs, obviously has huge benefits. Some of these benefits and advantages of specific weaponry are outlined below:

+ The advent of smaller, lighter, high-capacity (able to carry a size-able amount of ammunition) pistols has meant that it is easier for a CPO to carry around more firepower that is easily conceal-able and has the benefit of a high level of reliability.

+ Improvements in ballistic body amour (bulletproof vests) and protective accessories (e.g., bulletproof briefcases[12]) are readily available to CPOs. When such equipment is used effectively it can assist as an effective risk reduction tool.

+ The proliferation of combat torches and miniature, high-power handheld torches makes the carrying and use of necessary equip-ment far easier than outdated, bulky, and less-powerful torches. This makes them easier for CPOs to carry and are more effective (brighter torches that last longer) to use than older models.

+ Improvements in communications equipment (see above sec-tion on communication). Smaller lighter radios and cell phones that last longer are obviously useful to CPOs when on long-term contracts.

---

[12] Carrying ballistic protection in any form could have huge benefits if an attack were to take place. Having everyday objects such as briefcases that are actually bullet-proof could be very useful for CPOs since they serve the dual purpose of a carrying case and protection device.

- Folding tactical batons such as the Armament Systems & Procedures (ASP) extendable baton provide an easy to carry alternative force option for CPOs. This means that the CPO could have the advantage of being able to carry a baton concealed and utilize it as a full-length baton if necessary to implement a force option lower than a firearm.

- Improvements in pepper sprays and mace mean that the potential for permanent damage to an assailant is minimized while the capacity to stop him from attacking is increased. This is also an excellent minimum force option as compared to the firearm.

- The improvements in combat folder knives (these are knives where the blade folds in and out of the handle), which are available in many sizes and weights making personal choice possible for CPOs when selecting a bladed weapon. These improvements make it easy for a CPO to carry a combat-effective knife in comfort. It also provides the CPO with an additional force option other than the firearm.

- Flexi-cuffs such as the Armament Systems & Procedures (ASP) Trifold are light and easy to use and eliminate the necessity for CPOs to carry heavier steel and more cumbersome handcuffs.

- Utility tools (such as the Leatherman multi-tool) are easy to carry and have many different tools (pliers, screwdrivers, etc.) that could be useful to CPOs.

Trends regarding other close protection-related equipment

There are many tools that are utilized by CPOs while operational that are not necessarily weapons. These tools could assist in various aspects such as planning or monitoring the protection team during an operation. Several of these are outlined below:

- Use of computers – Basic computer skills (Internet, e-mail and report writing) are a vital operational skills requirement for CPOs in this day and age.

- Use of electronic security measures (cameras, alarms, infrared beams, and access control measures) have improved greatly in terms of sophistication and technological advancement over the last few years. It is therefore important for any CPO to have, at the very least, a basic understanding of these tools since they form an important part of ensuring a VIP's safety at work or residences.

- It is necessary for a CPO to have a basic understanding of the way that electronic surveillance takes place and the **complexities involved**. In most cases a CPO will make use of professionals in the field of **electronic counter measures (ECM)** in order to negate or minimize the risks associated with information security or breaches thereof.

◆ Improvements in vehicle tracking systems now means that a team leader or operation room controller can simultaneously keep track of all vehicular movements during a close protection operation. This makes the overall coordination of the close protection operation far easier. It would also enable better logistical support for field operatives since it would be simpler (than in the past) for the coordinator to know where the CPO team is. This has also been extended to utilizing such technologies for people tracking.

◆ The proliferation and widespread availability Global Positioning Systems (**GPS**) has made navigation and orientation (during route planning and operations) infinitely simpler and can dramatically cut down the time spent on the planning of VIP venue transfers and route reconnaissance phases of an operation. It can save both time and money since it **minimizes the risks of getting lost**.

Accessories

There are several other pieces of equipment that are relevant to the close protection industry as a whole (both training and operations). Several of these are outlined below:

◆ The use of digital and video cameras makes training and student feedback infinitely more effective (the student can have an opportunity to **actually see and rate their own performances in training**).

◆ It also can vastly improve the **quality** and **usability** of information gathered in **security audits** (see Appendix: Definitions) by having visual references to include in reports or the need to clarify certain points during team briefings (by having visual references to illustrate key points).

◆ Availability of fire-retardant material (such as Proban and Nomex) as well as small but highly effective fire extinguishers have made the task of reducing the risks of fire far easier, therefore enhancing the safety of the Principal.

◆ Improvements in first-aid equipment (e.g., portable defibrillators) mean that the protection team has less to carry (compact and lighter kits and equipment) and can achieve better results, if first aid has to be administered, than may have been possible in the past when such equipment was not readily available. The size and weight of modern equipment means that it can actually be carried with the CPO team. This obviously is very beneficial; if the equipment that is needed is on hand, then the Principal may not have to be evacuated to a hospital—thus, in some cases, lessening further endangerment enroute and possibly at the hospital itself.

Conclusion – Summary of Key Points

The importance for CPOs to be able to apply effective interpersonal communication while taking protocol into account cannot be overstated. It is also vital that a CPO can communicate effectively using the relevant communication tools such as cell phones and handheld radios. Aside from standard applications during operations, he/she needs these skills in order to elicit the assistance of relevant parties. This is especially so if these parties are able to smooth the running of a protection operation or enhance the safety of the Principal during such an operation.

It is also important to assess how communication is affected during an attack on Principal (AOP) situation. Much training needs to be done in order to ensure that a CPO team can function effectively as a unit under the duress of an attack situation. This involves extensive repetitive practice and rehearsal as well as ensuring that all communications are as clear, understandable, and as short and simple as possible. This would enable the effective communication of the close protection team member's actions in as short a period as possible.

Technology, such as the ease of access to the Internet, has had a tremendous impact on the way that close protection operations are conducted. Improved (in terms of size, weight, portability, technological features, and reliability) communications equipment has positively influenced close protection operations.

This can be seen throughout the operation, from the information gathering stages to the debriefing and termination stages. Improvements in close protection equipment and weaponry now mean that a CPO has the capacity to carry equipment that has better performance than in the past (e.g., carrying of high-capacity, small frame semi-automatic pistols like the Glock 19 or 26). This allows a CPO to, in fact, carry more ammunition while having less overall equipment weight and, therefore, be better able to conceal his/her weaponry, i.e., less bulky than previous equipment/firearms.

It is every CPO's and trainer's responsibility to keep as up-to-date as possible with changing trends and technological enhancements related to the close protection industry.

This is important in order to make the provision of protection services more effective, as well as improving on CPO's existing skills and competencies. In many cases better equipment translates directly to being able to provide the Principal with much better protection.

CHAPTER 8

USE OF FORCE OPTIONS AND CLOSE PROTECTION

"In many situations CPOs cannot, for legal or safety reasons, utilize their firearms or even get to them in time during a close range attack; therefore, they need to have other options, such as unarmed combat or batons."
—Lourens Jacobs

Introduction

Force options other than firearms would primarily include unarmed combat and improvised and alternative weaponry. In many countries only service personnel CPOs (e.g., police and military) may operate with firearms, with the result that most civilian CPOs operating in such an environment would need to focus their training on other force options.

It would make sense that CPOs moving from the military or police into the private sector would have been trained in one of the services' close protection units. CPOs with this training would therefore apply the same use of force strategies that they were trained on in their previous units. In other words, since most service personnel were and still are trained in a firearms-reliant manner, a CPO with this background may be limited in the use of force options that he/she could effectively apply.

Moreover, the vast majority of close protection trainers who became civilian instructors utilize the training methodology with which they are familiar. This methodology is also based primarily on what was taught in the various government-associated agencies that were running close protection details. The doctrine for almost all of these is to be reliant on the use of firearms during attack situations. This doctrine still holds true for protection of high-risk personnel, as in all likelihood, if a protection detail must respond to attack in such a situation, it is probably a maximum force situation

An identified hindering factor that accompanies firearm reliance is that the situations in which a CPO could safely utilize his or her firearm are few and far between, taking into account situational and safety factors of the protection team, the Principal, and the general public.

In addition a further question that arises is whether the majority of CPOs operating today, actually have sufficient training to competently handle their firearms under the pressures of an attack situation in which innocent civilians may be hurt by misplaced shots or over penetration.[13]

While the concept of applying unarmed combat or alternative weaponry as minimum force options seems straightforward, the wider issue seems to be whether individual CPOs actually know when to use the available different force options. This is as a universal problem being faced by service and civilian security personnel. The controversy over applied force in self-defense becomes more obvious as the concept of "use of minimum force" is a key aspect needing to not only be understood but also applied in all violent situations.[14]

The author, left, and Dr. Dennis Hanover 10ᵗʰ Dan demonstrating integration between firearms and unarmed combat.

This chapter aims to look at the reasons why training in force options other than the use of firearms is needed. Steps necessary to implement unarmed combat and alternative weaponry into the core training of close protection personnel will be examined. This is vital so

---

[13] Over penetration is the term used to describe a projectile that not only enters its designated target but passes straight through it. Over penetration could be dangerous to innocent bystanders behind the target as the bullet may still be traveling at a high enough speed to cause death or injury.

[14] For more information see: Mistry et al, 2001 *The Use of Force by Members of the South African Police Service: Case Studies From Seven Policing Areas in Gauteng.*

that a CPO can respond with the correct level of force in any given violent encounter. Responding with the correct force option needs to be an instinctive process since under the intensity of attack there is usually not time to decide on what the best course of action should be or what level of force the response should be.

Definitions

Some key concepts relating to unarmed combat, self defense, and alternative weaponry will be clarified below:

- Unarmed combat refers to the use of force by a CPO to restrain or incapacitate an attacker without the use of a firearm or alternative weapon.
- Alternative weaponry refers to the use of any tool or implement other than a firearm or unarmed combat that can be used to incapacitate or restrain an attacker.
- Improvised weaponry will refer to the use of everyday objects in a CPO's surroundings that could be used as a weapon or for distraction.
- The concept of self-defense implies that relevant weapons or tools are utilized in the defense of oneself, i.e., there is a direct threat to your physical well-being by other parties.

Background to the Use of Minimum Force Concept

"Use of force" is a topic currently surrounded by a good deal of controversy. This seems to be true for all parties affected by various use-of-force legislation or regulations. The debate on "use of force" impacts, in various ways, on all parties involved in the close protection industry, whether it is a CPO claiming that he/she has the right to utilize any means necessary to protect his or her client or the client claiming that he or she does not want firearms and violence around.

A detailed list of examples illustrating the misconceptions regarding use of force could be provided but for the purposes of this book, use of force will concentrate on the concept outlined as:

> *"In order for a response to be considered one of minimum*
> *force the defender (CPO) must respond with only that*
> *amount of force necessary to stop the threat and/or create*
> *enough time for the Principal to be safely evacuated."*
> —Clinton McGuire

When assessing minimum force from the point-of-view of CPO training and operations it is important that a comprehensive understanding of the overall close protection initiative is in place. Thorough understanding of the law regarding use of force is something that cannot be ignored since a CPO who merely stops an attacker from harming the Principal may not be sufficient. *It must be done in accordance with the law.*

This may seem simple enough, but the reality is that the CPO must decide and execute an effective and legal response to an attack situation under immense pressure. The time that a CPO has to decide on the correct reaction in any situation can probably be counted in split seconds (i.e., the need for split-second decision making). It would therefore be justified to state that a CPO's reactions must be planned in advance and trained to be as instinctive as possible under the duress and confusion of an attack. If this is not done on an ongoing basis then the wrong decision may be made, especially if responses are not drilled into a CPO's subconscious to become a learned and instinctive (spontaneous but correct) response at the same time.

It is an accepted fact that the use of a firearm in response to an attack is usually considered a maximum force reaction. However, in the past, most close protection operations were run by the police or similar agencies. If use of force was warranted, it would probably be because a definite attack on a high-profile person was taking place. This would necessitate the use of maximum force in retaliation (i.e., application of firearms).

An example of this affecting service CPOs is the case of South African government close protection units. The altering of the "use of force" during arrest[15] has meant that police officers are as limited in response to violent attack as civilians (i.e., can only be utilized if a life-threatening situation arises). Accordingly if a maximum force response is utilized by police, there may be serious consequences (if the officer involved is found to have used excessive force, he/she may be prosecuted for his or her actions) after the situation has occurred.

The bottom line is that the concept of minimum force has gained more acceptance and become a guiding principle with regard to the use of force, specifically deadly force.

Consequently minimum force is applicable to all CPOs whether service personnel or civilians. Probably one of the most effective ways to deal with the legal aspects and associated limitations on the use of force is to train the close protection operative to have rounded skills (the ability to apply various force options to deal with a violent situation).

The Need for CPOs to Possess Rounded Skills
"Rounded skills" refer to a CPO who is sufficiently trained to posses the relevant range of force options. He/she needs to be able to apply the cor-

---

[15] This is found in Section 49 of the Criminal Procedure Act 51 of 1977 but has been changed in the Judicial Matters Amendment Bill introduced on February 1, 2004 (B2-2005).

rect level of force in an attack situation, while **taking into consideration** not only the **law** but the **safety of the CPO** and **Principal** as well.

While considering this, it is clear that even though the CPO should be highly trained in the tactical use of firearms he/she is far more likely to utilize unarmed combat or alternative weaponry in an altercation. This would allow for minimizing the risks of using maximum force in a situation where a high-level force option may not be warranted.

The lack of rounded skills was illustrated, during a presentation on use of force options and alternative weaponry conducted by Dynamic Alternatives Pty Ltd. in March 2001, to over 80 active members of the Presidential Protection Unit and VIP Protection Services of the South African Police Service (SAPS). Staff of Dynamic Alternatives asked the officers attending the presentation the two following questions:

1. Have you ever utilized your firearm to defend a Principal against attack while providing close protection services?
2. Have you ever pushed, restrained, or had to strike [unarmed] someone while protecting a Principal as part of a close protection detail?

The response was clear: far more officers had used unarmed combat than firearms. Approximately 70 officers stated that they have had to use some sort of unarmed combat techniques while working as a member of a close protection detail, with only one officer claiming to have utilized his firearm while performing protection related duties. These responses were certainly interesting since, after further research, the vast majority of officers had received little if any unarmed combat and alternative weaponry training for their jobs as CPOs. It was also clear that the focus of all training that they had previously received concentrated on the use of firearms as the primary response to almost all attack situations.

Furthermore, almost all experts echoed the sentiments expressed above by these police members of close protection units. While most felt that it was necessary for CPOs to be well trained in the tactical usage of firearms, the vast majority were of the belief that unarmed combat and related skills training receive far less attention in training and retraining programs when compared to firearms skills.

> **The direct meaning of this, is that the way that most CPOs are trained does not correlate with the way that they are going to have to work and respond in real life situations. There appears to be a major imbalance in training methodology when assessing use of force.**

This will have to be adjusted in the future if a focus on practical out-comes-based training is to be achieved. A probable reason for CPOs and other security personnel not being able to effectively apply the concepts of minimum force may be attributed to the fact that these operatives have not been sufficiently trained in the use of force options other than firearms, nor do they appear to fully comprehend the implications of the use of force in particular deadly force utilizing firearms.

Situational Factors Affecting Use of Force

There are several factors that will affect what weaponry and level of force a CPO would choose in a given situation. These are discussed in more detail below.

Firearms usage at various different distances

After assessing various relevant literature sources including assassination case studies and training manuals, certain consistencies become apparent. Aspects worth noting include the fact that **the majority of close protection handgun-shooting incidents take place at a range of less than 8 meters, with many of them at less than 5 meters.** This indicates a disturbing trend in the way that CPOs are trained in comparison to what really happens. In several cases, what happened does not correlate with the way in which CPOs are trained to utilize their firearms and tactical defensive options during an AOP (attack on Principal). An example of this is the assassination of Yitzchak Rabin where he was shot and killed from only a couple of meters away.

A well-known—albeit slightly out of date, but still very relevant—training video titled, *Surviving Edged Weapons*, was made as an instructional tape for police officers in the United States and contains examples of **knife attacks on police officers,** demonstrated and verified **at an approximate range of 7 meters or less.** It was noted by police officers in the video that a committed attacker will be able to rush and stab an officer before the officer can draw and accurately fire his weapon. The implications are that at a range of 7 meters[16] or less it would probably be more beneficial for the CPO to utilize unarmed combat or alternative weaponry as a first option and only after that to then possibly draw the firearm if the situational variables allowed this action (Calibre Press video production).

In order for a CPO to be able to do this, an integrated approach to tactics and response to attack needs to be applied. Due to the complexities of responding to an attack situation, it is clear that if a CPO is not

---

[16] In the publication *The Modern Bodyguard*, the following information is given: "FBI summary of officers killed, together with police gunfight data has remained consistent—92% of all fire-fights occur within 20 feet." (Consterdine: 230).

trained to integrate relevant unarmed combat and associated techniques with drawing and firing a firearm, then, in many cases, the response would be too late or ineffective. The end result may be injury or death to the CPO and/or Principal.

It is also a well-known fact that under the intensity of attack, the human flight-or-fight instinct triggers adrenal dump (a huge injection of adrenalin into the body). This adrenal dump will cause, among other side effects, disorientation and inhibited judgment of space/distance perception. This means that during training, realistic situations need to be simulated in order for the trainee to be able to learn to assess and utilize the right tools based on the distance of attack while under the induced pressure of the simulation.

Crowds and working environment effects on use of force
The situations where CPOs can safely utilize their firearms effectively are few and far between. When analyzing the reasoning behind this trend, the following factors can be identified:

1. In many close protection-related situations that might warrant the use of force, the most common identified environment was that of working in a crowd. Any armed response in a crowded situation has the inherent risk of the CPO shooting non-combatants (e.g., bystanders). This is an obvious example of the risks of utilizing a firearm in terms of safety and efficiency.

2. The next problem is the fact that in an attack situation it is not always possible to see what is behind your attacker. This means that over-penetration of shots fired could kill or injure innocent civilians.

The author, front left, working on a high-profile protective detail in West Africa. (Note the crowd, which could make using firearms difficult.)

3. In order to counter this concern many CPOs carry hollow point-type[17] ammunition. However, this still leaves the problems of accurate shooting and ricochets that could injure or kill innocent civilians.

There is also the problem of weapon retention. While working in a crowded area it may be difficult for a CPO to both draw and fire his weapon as the crowd may overwhelm him and take his/her weapon. It is a common rule for CPOs that when working in a crowd, they may lose jewelry and other objects on their person. Many CPOs carry retention holsters (holsters with a retention clip or similar mechanism) for such situations. These holsters may slow the drawing of a firearm slightly but makes retention of the undrawn weapon much easier.

Identified Training Inadequacies in Close Protection

When all of the aspects outlined above are considered, the problems posed by use of firearms in crowds and the resultant risks of over penetration or missing cannot be ignored. However, these problems can be rectified through ongoing and intensive training. In assessments on CPOs conducted by Dynamic Alternatives Pty Ltd., certain disturbing trends were identified. By evaluating these assessments,[18] the following findings were noted.

1. Most of the assessed CPOs were of the opinion that they could utilize their firearms effectively under pressure. However over 50% could not pass the evaluations[19] on the first attempt.

2. Much ongoing training, retraining, and practice is necessary to maintain required operational standards. The vast majority of close protection personnel researched were of the opinion that their peers had neither the time nor the inclination to put in the necessary "range time" in order to maintain the level of competency necessary to utilize their firearms in close protection-related attack situations.

---

[17] Hollow point ammunition (for example the Winchester SXT) is designed to expand and adjust shape when entering a human attacker, thereby slowing down and lodging in the assailant and causing maximum physiological damage. This is referred to as the bullet's ability for "one shot stop," in other words, the bullet is quite likely to stop an attacker with one accurate, well-placed shot.

[18] These assessments were conducted on over 50 CPOs who underwent close protection and related tactical firearms assessments in South Africa during the period November 2003 to May 2004 .

[19] These evaluations comprised of basic firearm handling skills, i.e., draw and fire, rapid fire, turning and firing, hand and magazine changes, etc., as well as two CPO-related shooting drills—one providing cover for a Principal and the other simulating the evacuation of a Principal while providing covering fire.

Two apparent problems were identified by the assessors concerning the poor performance of the CPOs who were evaluated during this process. Firstly, the CPOs were not initially trained effectively with regard to the necessary competencies of close protection related firearms usage. Secondly, the candidates assessed may have been trained effectively but did not retrain often enough to maintain the required level of competency. Both of these problems can be addressed through the establishment of a compulsory industry minimum standard with regularly implemented competency evaluations.

Moreover, another identified problem related to the assessments mentioned above was that very little unarmed combat training was undertaken by most CPOs evaluated.

There was also a cause for further concern in that many of the assessed candidates claimed to have undergone some sort of martial arts training. This prior training was meant for them to achieve competency in unarmed combat tactics as applied to close protection. The vast majority of candidates assessed who claimed such backgrounds did not outperform their competitors, who in some cases had little or no unarmed combat or martial arts experience. Whether or not martial arts prepare CPOs for the demands of close protection work will be discussed below:

Martial Arts and Close Protection

The link between Close Protection and martial arts is frequently exaggerated. The effectiveness of many martial arts in the specialist security world is often questioned. In their book *Bodyguarding: A Complete Manual*, Rapp and Lesce explain this concept as follows:

> *"Karate schools tend to train students for competition,*
> *not defense against deadly threat. They also concentrate*
> *on developing style, rather than quick economical*
> *and disabling blows and holds."*
> —Rapp & Lesce: 23

By definition the term "martial art" means that some of the system is "martial" and some is "art." The initial aim of all combative systems was to train its proponents to deal with the harsh realities of life and death combat. However, in this day and age many of these combat systems adapted from their initial functions to become methods of self-development for their proponents, or for sports, with the combative concepts becoming secondary. This can be clearly seen in the names of such arts as Jujitsu, which means "gentle art," being adapted by Jigaro Kano in the 1920s to become Judo or "gentle way." While the change may seem small, the focus was on transforming a combat system into a platform for self-development and sport.

> *When it comes to defending the life of a Principal against violent attack, a CPO must not only have the capability to effectively defend him/herself but also the Principal that he/she is protecting.*

In order to have the skills necessary to provide effective protection the need for competency in unarmed and alternative weapon defense is vital.[20] As a direct result of the fact that a CPO may have limited time available for training and retraining, the focus of such training should be on practical easy to learn and apply skills. Any system or technique employed by a CPO must meet certain criteria in order to be considered effective. These criteria are as follows:

1. The techniques must be based on the realities of attack and in line with the modus operandi of the way in which attackers actually engage their victims. All too often, techniques taught in martial arts systems are based on what the instructor perceives to be real as opposed to **what actually happens in a violent attack**. Moreover, these techniques are usually practiced in such a controlled and unrealistic environment that they do not resemble the actual real-life situations the CPO needs to be training for.

2. The techniques that are taught to CPOs **need to be simple and forgiving** (i.e., not compromise the CPO if the technique does not work). If the techniques are too complicated to learn, the likelihood of them being applied in pressure situations is very slim. The concept of applying forgiving techniques is designed in order not to leave the CPO off-balance and open to counterattack if something goes wrong while performing the technique.

3. Self-defense techniques need to be **integrated into the close protection**-related use of firearms and easily applied with relevant CPO operational methodology (i.e. ,walking formations and IADs).

4. The fact that the CPO may be carrying a lot of equipment, may be tired, and **have several attackers to deal with at the same time**, must be taken into account when assessing the applicability of self-defense techniques or tactics.

5. The CPO must have the capability to **fight off attackers under any circumstance**, at any distance, and in any environment since

---

[20] To emphasize the importance for a CPO to have good, unarmed combat skills in the United Kingdom, Peter Consterdine states: "When it comes to the bottom line, you have to be able to fight and remember, you are seldom if ever going to be armed, certainly never if you work in this country [United Kingdom] and seldom, even if abroad. You are dependent on your physical unarmed skills, aggression training and fitness." (Consterdine: 271)

the attacker is likely to engage when the CPO is least prepared to deal with the situation (*i.e., attackers exploit opportunities*).

*CPOs training in defensive tactics.
(Note that the training is being done on a shooting range,
with the CPOs carrying weapons, with no mats.)*

Several ideas on how CPOs could work around the difficulties of gaining access to firearms were presented during the interviews but almost all of the respondents who had operated internationally were in agreement that the ability to fight unarmed and/or utilize improvised weapons was vital for CPOs in order for them to effectively operate internationally.

Conclusion – Summary of Key Points

There is a clear need for a shift in the way that CPOs train and operate. The focus needs to shift from being firearms reliant to CPOs having rounded combat skills that include unarmed combat, use of alternative weaponry, and improvised weaponry. Currently most training programs cover firearms responses to attack in much detail, but pay very little attention to other force options. Some training courses do not touch on any of these skills at all.

It is important to note that even though there are certain links between martial arts and close protection, they are not always congruent. Several key issues were identified that outlined what would make a self-defense technique applicable in terms of close protection requirements. Some of these concepts focused on aspects such as complex techniques that are simple and easy to learn. This is vital if these techniques are to be applied under the duress of an attack situation. It is also important that unarmed combat and alternative weaponry skills are integrated with tactical firearms skills and close protection practices.

Changes in use-of-force legislation as well as the improbability of being able to carry weapons internationally, means that a CPO needs to have various reactive capabilities in order to comply with legal guidelines. This implies that a CPO needs to be up-to-date with any relevant changes in applicable legislation. A CPO needs to not only have a thorough understanding of relevant law but also be able to apply the law in practical, work-related situations.

In order for CPO trainees to actually have a workable understanding of the legislation, training needs to focus on an outcomes-based approach. This needs to include scenario- and example-related training for students so they can learn to apply their knowledge in actual working situations. There is also a definite need for the CPO to concentrate on preventative planning and to implement a proactive approach in order to avoid threatening situations. This approach should be outlined and included in all training programs. This is vital if CPOs are to be able to "hold their own" in the international arena.

CHAPTER 9

FORWARD THINKING, ADAPTABILITY, AND THE NEED FOR A PROACTIVE APPROACH TO CLOSE PROTECTION

*"The problem is action is always faster than reaction.
Therefore, we prefer to take a proactive rather than
a reactive approach to bodyguarding."*
—King: 29

Introduction

The concept of being proactive and avoiding potentially threatening situations is the mainstay of any competent close protection professional. There is a need to not only be able to predict the likelihood (the when and how) of a threat occurring, but to also implement the necessary measures to either avoid or limit the level of exposure of the Principal to such threats.

Proactive planning is no longer a task that can be solely delegated to other parties (such as a designated planning officer). The CPO must have the skills to implement effective, risk-management practices both prior to and during a close protection operation. The importance for a CPO to be able to think on his/her feet is vital. This is because during an operation the Principal's itinerary may constantly change and it will be the job of the CPOs on the ground to implement the adjusted advance planning.

The specialist subfield of risk management, threat identification, threat avoidance, as well as comprehensive planning skills needs to go hand in hand with a flexible and adaptable approach. What this means, is that it is **not enough to predict what is likely to happen in a given** *circumstance and then plan for that. It is possible that situations will occur that, regardless of how comprehensive the planning was, were not factored into the operation/situation. In these scenarios, it comes down to the CPO on the ground having the correct mindset, skill, and experience to manage the situation.*

The nature of close protection work combined with the huge number of variables that may unexpectedly occur, reinforce the need for all CPOs to have proactive planning skills. Today's CPO must not only have the skills needed to plan ahead but must also possess the lateral and quick-thinking ability to effectively avoid and manage almost any situation under extreme stress. This concept was constantly mentioned throughout this book but has not yet been explained in enough detail to validate the relevance of this point. A breakdown and more detailed explanation will be covered in this chapter that will hopefully assist in bridging the identified gap.

Forward-Thinking CPOs

> *"In close protection the attacker has almost all the advantages. One of the only things that can help to deal with this problem is to be proactive and take measures to prevent an attack from happening."*
> —David M. Sharp

The concept of forward thinking can be explained as "the ability to process available information and then predict the likelihood of different variables occurring in a given scenario."

An example of applied forward thinking could be a CPO who must take his/her Principal to the airport. It is not enough to simply know the relevant routes and pick-up and drop-off times. The CPO must attempt to predict as many aspects as possible that may form a barrier to the successful completion of the task (such as traffic jams, flat tires, possible car accidents, all attack scenarios and how to manage them, etc).

When looking at the definition of close protection, the three primary objectives need constantly to be taken into account, namely: to ensure the Principal's safety, peace of mind, and physical comfort. The CPO must effectively predict the applicable variables relevant to each of these aspects as thoroughly as possible. Moreover, proactive measures should then be taken to avoid any of these problems, or at the very least, limit the potential of these problems occurring.

It is an exceptionally difficult task to attempt to predict many of the contingencies that may occur. To be able to do this a CPO needs to have had a wide range of close protection-related experience, in which he/she was exposed to many variables and situations. The fact that it is difficult to gain such a level of experience means that there are not many CPOs capable of functioning as a specialist planning officer.

However, in many operations there is not an allocated budget for a specialist planning officer's services to be utilized. Therefore, the CPO on the ground would have to perform all the necessary planning. This would mean that regardless of whether a CPO is an experienced planning officer or not, he/she should, at the very least, be competent to conduct basic planning and operations to survive various scenes and safeguard the Principal.

Perhaps the most effective way to deal with not having a set planning officer is to ensure that during training a practical, comprehensive, and realistic approach to planning is not just taught but ingrained in potential CPOs. This would mean that, as a basic competency, a CPO would need to be able to conduct rudimentary planning which should include the following:

+ advance work and liaison
+ Principal profiling
+ threat assessment and risk analysis
+ determination of IADs and contingency plans.

Effective, applicable planning consumes both time and resources. However, the benefits of this exercise cannot be over emphasized. There is a wide selection of planning and risk management documents available in various manuals and applicable literature. However, the concept of simply taking a pro-forma planning document and applying it would not be a very effective approach. There are many reasons why the use of someone else's pro-forma documents is not suggested (e.g., there may be either too much or not enough detail, etc.). This becomes especially relevant in the private sector where time, manpower, and budget constraints are applicable.

A more recommended approach to planning would be to utilize a pro-forma document in conjunction with a well-trained planning team that has the ability to predict any potentially threatening occurrences. These predictions would be based on collection of all relevant information, followed by detailed analysis of this information. This information would then be superimposed on the principal profile and linked to his itinerary. The process would then involve a prioritization of the identified threats and determination of ways to either avoid these threats or minimize the likelihood of them occurring (in many cases, experienced CPOs have pro-forma documents that would be **adjusted and tailored as necessary for each task**).

This planning process should run in a continuous looping system. It is a fundamental error to conduct planning prior to an operation and then consider the process complete.

This is important since even if changes to the Principal's itinerary, both in times and locations, are factored into the security planning for the venues, routes, and resulting time frame changes, they would in all probability have been impossible to consider.

Therefore, a planning or advance team may have to be quickly dispatched to gather the necessary information. Once the information has been analyzed, a quick assessment and possible reassessment of the threat minimization plan needs to be developed.

The Need for Thinking-Adaptable Protectors

"The ability for an operative to think on his [her] feet and do the correct thing in all situations is vital."
—David M. Sharp

The term "adaptability" refers to a CPO's ability to adjust and effectively react to quickly changing variables in their environment. This means not only being able to fit into the environment in which they must operate but also be able to effectively protect a person while adapting to a changing situation. Furthermore, it is not simply the capability to cope with adverse conditions but to process complicated, potentially life-threatening occurrences and then quickly implement the correct counter-action(s).

During the in-depth interviews conducted while researching this book, experts were asked to list the necessary skills that a CPO must posses to be able to operate effectively. The concept of a CPO being adaptable, as well as being able to think on his/her feet, is listed in the top three close protection operational requirements "because people's lives may depend on it." This reinforces the concept that a CPO's operational skills requirements, although broad, are vital in order to perform the necessary activities needed to protect someone's life or more specifically to keep the Principal safe and out of harms way.

As a direct result of the nature of close protection work, as well as the diversity of Principals that a CPO may have to protect, he/she may very well find themselves at an embassy party or political rally on one day and in the bush the next. An effective CPO should be able to blend into all relevant environments. To achieve this takes not only effective training but the CPO must also have the correct physical and mental attributes for this specialized field.

According to the previously mentioned job description of a CPO, he/she must protect the integrity of a Principal not just his/her physical well-being. To achieve this may mean something as simple as preventing a waiter form spilling a drink on the Principal or something as complicated as creating layers of security and access control measures to minimize the chances of attackers being able to get physically close to the Principal.

Another interesting trend identified during the interview process was that CPOs with a military or police background sometimes appear to have trouble adjusting to the demands and operational skills requirements of the private sector. The reasoning behind this observation focused on two primary concepts. Firstly, the difficulty in accessing additional resources; and secondly, the fact that in some cases these CPOs only performed specialized functions of close protection while in the police or military. These two aspects will be explained in more detail below.

Limited access to resources refers to the fact that in the majority of cases service personnel would have had access to resources such as CAT teams, intelligence information, or even counter-snipers while operating in the police or military.

This differs substantially from how things are usually conducted in the private sector where a protection detail may be given a set budget (usually quite small) to utilize for the entire operation irrespective of the fact that the operational team may feel that more resources are required in order to provide effective protection. The bottom line in private sector close protection is that services are rendered with a close eye cast on making money for the service provider company or with a limited expenditure because the client does not want to pay more. Whereas often in state close protection services "no costs are spared," especially when protecting high-profile, politically sensitive VIPs.

The concept of job specialization goes hand-in-hand with the fact that service personnel usually have access to more state resources than their civilian counterparts do. In many of the close protection operations that are run by the police or military, there may be enough operatives on the detail to allow for set (static) placement of CPOs. This means that military or police operatives may work in only one designated position of a protection detail for the majority of their service career. What often happens when such CPOs begin to work in the private sector is that they struggle to adapt to working with limited resources and the fulfilling of multiple functions on a close protection detail themselves.

It may take such CPOs some time to gain the experience to effectively adapt to this different working environment.

How to Implement a Proactive Approach

"The ability to minimize risk by being able to predict what may go wrong and implement contingency plans or remove the source of the problem is a vital skill for all planning officers to possess."
—Clinton McGuire

Adopting a proactive approach through planning and fieldwork is definitely not a new concept in the fields of specialist security and close protection. The concept of detailed planning and gathering of information is usually referred to as advance work (see earlier chapter covering the Secure Advance Party).

By definition, advance work entails:

+ gathering information before an operation,
+ analyzing this information, and
+ utilizing the results to preemptively plan to avoid the identified, potentially threatening situations. Probably the key aspect of this proactive cycle would be the determination of what can actually be done in order to directly avoid or minimize the exposure of the protection detail to these identified threatening situations.

It is not necessary for a CPO or designated planning officer to be an expert in human behavior and psychology in order to plan effectively. However, it is vital that a CPO has at least a fundamental understanding of human behavior and psychology. **The CPO's ability to forecast human behavior (the potential attacker's actions) in different contexts and situations is a vital component to being proactive.** This is necessary in order to be able to plan ahead as well as forecast what variables may affect the smooth running of a close protection operation and then plan accordingly to manage these variables.

The last aspect identified as a key factor in having a proactive approach is to understand what the level of training and necessary reactions a protection team should have. A CPO or planning officer must have the ability to be able, in advance, to predict the formations, positions, mental state, and reactionary capabilities of a close protection team. This is vital since when planning for contingencies, if these factors are not taken into account, it may mean that the actual application of the plan may not be realistic.

In close protection where people's lives may depend on planning, it is important for this approach to be consistently applied towards the manner in which all planning is conducted. When taking the above into account, it can be understood that the better the CPO is at applying "forward thinking" with insight, the less he/she exposes his/her Principal to potentially dangerous, uncomfortable or threatening situations. CPOs would severely limit their chances of a successful and incident free operation if they do not apply forward thinking and proactive planning for all possible scenarios.

Reactive Aspects

The concept of reflexive reaction to different situations shows what threats and attack situations a CPO should be trained to deal with. There is, however, quite a bit of differentiation about what is and what is not perceived as a priority skill by the different experts. The concept of reactionary aspects will be broken down and analyzed in the paragraphs that follow.

CPOs "embusing" a Principal.
(Note that the door of the vehicle is open and the vehicles are running; also, the follow vehicle is in a position where it creates additional cover and could drive off if necessary.)

The term "reactive" refers to the idea that there has been or there is about to be some sort of occurrence that may require specific action from an individual CPO or close protection team. CPO's reactions can be subdivided into the following subcategories:

+ The trained reflexes a CPO must have to be able to respond immediately to attack situations
+ What instinctive reflex a CPO needs to posses
+ A CPO's adaptability to diverse conditions.

The concept that one objective can be achieved through different means is also relevant to CPO reactions and will be included in the discussions below.

Trained and Instinctive Reflexes of CPOs

Trained reflexes refer primarily to the pre-determined immediate action drills (IADs) in which all CPOs should be competent. There should be IADs in place for the majority of contingencies that would have been identified during the advance work and planning stages of an operation.

The close protection operative and/or team should be able to respond fluently and reflexively in order to provide the best possible protection for a Principal should a potentially dangerous situation actually occur. Below is a summarized list of situations for which a CPO should train IADs. It is by no means a complete list but should provide the reader with an overview of what should be required of a competent CPO. The list of situational IADs is as follows:

- firearm attack close range (handgun or assault rifle)
- firearm attack long range
- knife attack
- unarmed attack (striking, grabbing, or tackling)
- hand grenade
- suspicious object/improvised explosive device (IED)
- various vehicle ambushes (roadblock, rolling box attack, etc.)
- friendly crowds (swarming and mobbing the Principal)
- unfriendly crowds (rioting, throwing objects, etc.)
- potential injury to the Principal from environmental factors (such as tripping or falling)
- medical emergency (heart attack, choking, etc.)

Self Test

Name 10 IADs

An ideal standard for the close protection industry and for a CPO to be considered competent in IADs would be based on the CPO having at least the *ability and skills to react in the correct manner during any of the above situations*. While there may be several possible reactions to any one of the above situations, the correct reaction would be that reaction which provides the maximum safety to the Principal, the other members of the team, the individual CPO and the public.

Key Principles

1. Ability & skills to react in the correct manner
2. Protection of the Principal is the primary objective

The reactions should protect the parties in that order with the protection of the *Principal being the primary objective* and the safety of the public being the last. All of these reactions should be performed while simultaneously considering all the legal ramifications pertaining to an action.

Instinctive reflex would usually refer to the human "flight or fight" instincts, as well as to physiological and psychological factors that affect the human body during survival-based situations. Through effective and ongoing training most of the associated negative side-effects of adrenal release (see previous chapter) can be minimized enabling the CPO to respond effectively according to the correct trained response. In other words, through ongoing, effective scenario and reality-based training, the correct IAD (trained response) will actually become instinctive. Experience would also contribute to making IADs reflexive and instinctual.

Adaptability to Diverse Situations

> *"The one thing that you do not plan for will most probably be the thing that does [happen]."*
> —Lourens Jacobs

An attacker is most likely to study the movements of a Principal and attack in as unexpected manner as possible, usually when the protection team is least prepared to respond. It is for this reason that a CPO needs to have the capability to react according to instructions and/or trained cues. Moreover, he/she should be able to *very quickly assimilate* all relevant information, *weigh up* the relevant options, and *implement* the option that will provide the best possible outcome in terms of close protection objectives. This is perhaps not a skill that can be taught, but more of an inherent personality characteristic.

Key Principles

1. **Very quickly assimilate**
2. **Weigh up**
3. **Implement**

If a person's ability to adapt quickly to changing circumstance is more of a personality characteristic than a learned skill, effective selection and screening of potential CPOs becomes vital.[21] It would make sense to evaluate a potential CPO prior to conducting full training to assess whether he/she has the correct attributes to operate as a CPO.

It is obviously also possible to **enhance this attribute through realistic training** that simulates diverse situations. The more this is done under reality-based conditions, the more beneficial this training will be. It goes without saying that experience will condition a CPO more effectively than almost any alternative training method. There is, in fact, **no substitute for on-the-job experience.**

---

[21] This pre-evaluation/selection should assess a candidate's personality type and physical fitness, and ensure that he/she has no phobias or hindrances which could be a barrier to performing as a CPO. (For more information see section on Close Protection training and related issues.)

Achieving the Desired Outcome by Different Means

"We are in the business of finding solutions [to client prob-
lems], the client does not have to know how you get things
done—the point is that things [must] get done."
—Johan van Eck

Due to the diversity of situations with which a CPO may encounter, it is vital for him/her to have the ability to implement lateral thinking (think outside of the box). In other words, there may be several ways to deal with a problem and the most effective way may not seem to be the most obvious. This may not necessarily relate to an attack situation but how these are dealt with will affect the safety and smooth running of close protection operations.

An example of this could be as follows: "A client arrives at the airport at 10 p.m. and has an early morning television interview. The client's luggage does not arrive and the airline says it will only get there tomorrow evening."

There may be several options available to a CPO in order to deal with this situation and avoid inconvenience or embarrassment for the client. The CPO would probably first have to gather as much information as quickly as possible. He/she would than have to identify various courses of action and select the option that is the most effective from a safety and client preference point of view. The key concept is that CPOs may have to find solutions to many of the problems that a client may face.

The need to solve problems is something a CPO encounters every day but the problem is usually made more difficult to manage because of the limited time frames in which CPOs usually have to solve these problems and implement the solutions.

There are several methods of developing the
necessary skills but for the most part, problem-solving
and lateral thinking capability is something that a
potential CPO should posses before entering
the close protection industry.

Conclusion – Summary of Key Points

After collecting and analyzing all the relevant information a CPO must have the ability to forecast potentially threatening situations. However, just being able to do this is not enough. It is necessary for the CPO to determine and implement the most effective manner to avoid or minimize the Principal's and the protection team's exposure to these threats. In order to do this, a CPO must be able to apply the skills of forward thinking and advance planning. He/she must have the ability to quickly adapt to changes in the immediate environment. These skills need to extend into not only being able to determine what the correct reaction should be but what actually is possible in a given situation. A CPO's ability to do all of this would be based on his/her training and experience. A proactive approach should be adopted by all CPOs with the focus being on threat avoidance.

Moreover, the CPO should be able to reflexively respond to a threatening situation whether it was planned for or not. The reaction needs to be effected in such a manner as to maximize the safety of the Principal first and then that of the protection team members and public. The CPO should be trained to deal with, at the very least, a set of identified universal threats that include scenarios such as firearms attacks, medical emergencies, and hand grenade attacks. All natural instinctive flight or fight responses need to be practiced constantly and honed to the point where they work hand-in-hand with close protection-related IAD's.

Lastly, it should be an operational skills requirement for a CPO to be able to problem solve effectively under the intense stress sometimes encountered while providing protective services. While this is something that can be developed, if it is not an inherent personality characteristic, he/she probably has the wrong profile for close protection work.

The consensus of opinion of experts interviewed while researching this book indicated that pro-activity, effective planning ability, and the CPO's ability to **adapt** and **problem solve** are definitely key operational skills requirements. While a CPO may be able to work in the industry without all of the above competencies, he/she may not be operating at the level needed to ensure the complete safety of a Principal. Not all of the previously mentioned attributes can be considered learned skills; therefore, effective trainee selection (including evaluations on physical fitness, psychological profile and emotional suitability) is a vital component to ensure that the right people are being trained to perform close protection duties.

CHAPTER 10

RECOMMENDATIONS ON STANDARDS FOR CLOSE PROTECTION TRAINING

*Courage is resistance to fear, mastery
of fear—not absence of fear.*
—Mark Twain

Introduction

The aim behind the research project that formed the basis for this book was to determine the skills requirements necessary in order to formulate recommended standards for the further professionalization of the close protection industry. Throughout this book, recommendations have been given both from the author's point of view and from the statements made by industry experts. However, it is necessary to provide a skill-by-skill breakdown highlighting what recommended minimum competency standards could be implemented.

During the interviews portion of the research, experts were asked to give their opinions on what the minimum acceptable levels of competency should be for each of the identified skills that are needed to provide professional close protection services. In this chapter, these recommendations have been consolidated into a point-by-point overview. It should be noted that in many cases there are several options for implementation of standards and the recommendations given in this research are intended to serve only as guidelines.

During the in-depth interviews the experts were asked the following question and requested to comment on each subject:

"What kind of minimum standards would you set for the following criteria?"

+ prior educational qualifications
+ physical abilities

+ CPO skills
+ prior experience in guarding
+ firearm skills
+ unarmed combat
+ protective skills
+ first aid skills
+ security knowledge
+ advanced driver training
+ protocol and etiquette
+ management and business skills
+ related skills

The feedback and information gathered during the interviews was then correlated and grouped into relevant themes. The key aspects for each of the above-mentioned criteria are discussed below and should provide a guideline to measure standards for trainers as well as individuals who want to undergo a close protection training course.

Prior Educational Qualifications

The key concept being analyzed here is what level of education the prospective candidate should possess in order to be considered suitable for close protection training. The majority of respondents felt that the minimum should be Grade 12 (full completion of high school). The remaining respondents felt that a Grade 10 (partial completion of high school) would be sufficient. The point raised here was not so much the candidate's actual capability with literacy and numeracy, even though these are vital for a prospective CPO, but more importantly the candidate's level of "life experience."

The consensus seemed to be that a candidate should be around 21 years old with a valid Grade 12 certificate before entry into a basic training program could be considered. However, it was also universally expressed by the respondents that if the candidate was younger but showed the necessary commitment and maturity he/she should be accepted for training.

Additionally it was mentioned that a candidate should have some sort of military, police, or related security experience before being accepted into a close protection training program. Candidates without any previous experience could obtain basic security qualifications and experience as a bridge into the industry. This would be an acceptable base to begin close protection training. Prior experience was a point of concern in several interviews and is mentioned here simply as a point of consideration and not as a vital point of implementation.

Physical Abilities

> *"A rounded level of fitness that is regularly assessed is a*
> *vital aspect of a CPO's operational readiness."*
> —David M. Sharp

A point of controversy that was identified by most of the experts was the physical fitness and the physical competencies needed by a CPO in order to operate effectively. It was identified that not only is it necessary for the CPO to be fit enough to handle all operational situations (like an attack on the Principal) but it is most important for a CPO to look fit, i.e., have a fit appearance and to be in the necessary physical condition needed to deal with a violent attack. The reason for this is that in many cases appearance is one of the primary criteria that the Principal has on which to assess the CPO. This concept is mentioned in several literary sources but explained by Peter Consterdine as:

> *"Being a BG [bodyguard] is a specialist, demanding job if*
> *everything is done correctly and well and a correct attitude*
> *to fitness and training is integral to being able to 'switch on'*
> *and dig in when things get tough."*

A point often mentioned is that the fitness assessments done on CPOs need to be duty-related and not necessarily based on generic military or police assessments. The concept is that CPOs are best assessed based on skills they may have to perform. The example given was that it may be relevant for a CPO to carry a wounded client but not necessarily have to run 5 km within a specified time. Therefore, perhaps the fitness assessments should entail not only the generic push ups, pull ups, sit ups, and endurance runs, but also a dummy carry and agility course.

An example of a close protection related fitness assessment that could serve as a standard for a minimum level of competency could be as follows:

(Note: the evaluation should be done in a battery format with a two-minute allocated rest period between each exercise.)

- 45 push ups in 1 minute
- 40 sit ups in 1 minute
- 8 pull ups in 1 minute
- 6 x 50 m shuttle runs[22] (each alternate run should have the CPO carrying or dragging a 50 kg dummy)
- 2.4 km run in under 15 minutes
- 50 m swim in under 2 minutes

---

[22] Shuttle runs refers to running back and forth between two points that are 25 m apart.

The above assessment is merely an example of activities that could be utilized in an assessment and should not be considered the only valid method of assessing a CPO's physical competency. An obstacle course or similar agility assessment course could also be used to effectively measure a CPO's physical competency.

CPO Skills

CPO skills refer to the specific skills needed to perform close protection duties effectively. This is an extremely difficult topic to standardize. An example illustrating this could be: *if a CPO is being assessed on his/her planning skills, at what level should he/she actually be assessed (e.g., planning for a five-day operation with a 10-person protection detail or planning for a pick-up from the airport and drop-off at a hotel? There is an obvious distance between the planning/organizational levels needed for these different operations.)*

The subdivision of CPO skills is so broad that in order to simplify the relevant concepts, the four essential outcomes as identified earlier in this book have been chosen as a framework from which to expand. These serve only as examples based on indicators obtained from the research of what may be considered acceptable minimum competency standards. It would be unrealistic to explain as separate entities each and every individual competency relevant to close protection, as they function as a synergistic unit.

Self-Test

Can you complete a detailed principal profile, threat and risk assessment and design an operational itinerary?

It is therefore suggested that in order to try and formulate some form of set evaluation standards, that a guideline similar to the following be implemented:

+ All written documentation should be done on the basis of protecting a medium risk-level Principal. This could be clarified by outlining that there is definitely a threat but one that is not that likely to occur.

+ The planning and practical evaluations should consist of a team structure with a suggested minimum of three and a maximum of six team members as well as assessment of individual performance, i.e., 1-on-1 operation.

+ The operation to be planned for should be at least one-day long and should include protection of at least two different venues.

The first essential outcome **"determine the Principal's brief and risk profile,"** leaves a wide scope of options and tools available to demonstrate competency in this area. A recommended approach could be to highlight the key areas relevant to this competency and put them into a suggested set of documents and checklists. As a minimum these documents should include a risk and threat assessment, a principal profile and a detailed operational itinerary.

To demonstrate competency, a CPO should be able to compile each of the above documents in a workable format. There should be enough information in each document to compile an effective protection plan that would ensure the safety, well-being, and comfort of the Principal.

The second essential outcome is to **"Plan the transit/foot/venue protection operation of a Principal."** It should be noted that the essential outcomes should be conducted progressively as it would be impossible to plan for an operation without comprehensive information on the principal profile and the identified threats. In order to assess competency in this area, key concepts relevant to planning need to be demonstrated.

As a minimum, these planning documents should include, but not be limited to, the following:

- the written allocation of relevant resources
- a clear definition of roles and duties of team members
- a step-by-step breakdown of the different phases of the defined operation
- a summary of all necessary logistics required for the whole operation based on venues and transport
- a detailed set of contingencies and reactions to the identified threats that may occur, these should be correlated to the identified risk factors at different stages of a Principal's itinerary.

Key Principles

What planning documents should you be familiar with?

Regardless of the format in which all the above aspects are presented, it is vital that there is a structured approach to the planning and that the plan itself is practical and can actually be implemented. A written exam could also be used to assess a CPO's knowledge and understanding of all the relevant concepts.

The third essential outcome is to **"protect a Principal during transit/foot/venue movements and static situations."** In terms of evaluation, this could be done by utilizing a combination of practical assessments and scenario evaluations. The practical assessments should be based on a realistic scenario where the candidates should be able to demonstrate effective protection capabilities both as individuals and as members of a team. These scenarios should be performed in "live situations."

An example of this could be a shopping center where the candidate must demonstrate the relevant protective skills in a "live" environment.

At this stage, it is recommended, that only controlled "attacks"[23] are applied as the reactions of civilians or officials may endanger all parties. Key aspects to be assessed at this stage would include awareness, observation skills, positioning according to situation, and profile of the Principal as well as operation, teamwork, application of planning, and communication skills.

In terms of the actual physical protection of a Principal, the assessment should take place in a controlled environment like a shooting range or private training facility. The candidate should, at the very least, be able to demonstrate competency to effectively manage the following "Attack on Principal" situations:

+ long-range firearm attack (sniper)
+ close-range firearm attack (5–25 meters)
+ attack with a knife or similar weapon
+ suspicious object or IED
+ unarmed/grabbing attack
+ hand grenade attack
+ throwing of objects at the Principal (e.g., eggs)
+ dealing with "autograph seekers" and over-friendly persons

The candidate should be able to demonstrate the above in simulated scenarios where safety of all participants is the foremost concern. The assessments should include demonstration of effective embus and debus[24] methodology, effective demonstration of protective formations based on the scenario, and the ability to react effectively to anything that may occur.

The fourth essential outcome is for the CPO to demonstrate the ability to **"Terminate and review a protection operation."** This should include "feedback in verbal, written, and recorded formats." In terms of actual application, a candidate should be able to submit a detailed operational report explaining his/her role in the operation and making recommendations for the future. The candidate should also be able to verbally explain him/herself in a debriefing and justify all actions that were taken while operational. Assessment could include a question-and-answer session and the submission of an operational report, which should sufficiently demonstrate competency in this area. The format and layout is not as important as the content and should remain flexible.

---

[23] A simulated attack or ambush on the close protection detail.

[24] "Embus" and "Debus" refers to the manner in which a protection detail should escort a Principal into and out of a vehicle (i.e., embarking and disembarking). There are specific security related procedures that should be implemented during these activities which aim to minimize the exposure of the Principal.

Prior Experience in Guarding

The concept of a candidate having some sort of prior security-related experience before commencing with close protection training was mentioned earlier in this chapter. Prior experience is usually considered to be very helpful, but not absolutely essential, for a prospective candidate wanting to enter the industry. There are basically four types of candidate backgrounds that were identified as useful for someone who wants to be trained as a CPO to possess. These four backgrounds were:

+ military or related experience
+ police or related experience
+ security or related experience
+ martial arts and/or firearms experience

It should be stated that simply because a person has had experience in one or more of the above sectors, it does not necessarily mean that he/she is qualified to operate as a CPO.

Prior experience in one of these fields would simply be a good indicator that a person may have the potential to become a CPO.

Additionally, prior experience in the above areas could enable the initial close protection training period to be shorter since it will be easier to train a candidate with related experience to achieve the necessary competencies.

Firearm Handling and Related Skills

The reality is that the use of firearms is considered a maximum force option. Maximum force may be necessary when one correlates the core function of close protection, which is to protect a Principal's life. However, what is important to determine is what scope and depth of firearm skills competency does a CPO actually need to possess.

The basis for establishing competency should focus on a CPO's ability to handle a pistol. Use of assault weapons and shotguns would be a must if CPOs were planning to deploy in a hostile environment and could be done as add-on training.

The starting platform should include the following skills:

+ Handle handguns safely
+ Apply knowledge and understanding of the relevant legislation required
+ Operate, use, and maintain handguns
+ Shoot handgun competently—this should include as a minimum:
    + Shooting fundamentals (stance, grip, trigger squeeze, etc.)
    + Fault analysis (stoppage drills)
    + Low-light shooting

+ Basic movement and shooting positions (turn and shoot, standing, kneeling, prone, etc.)
+ Cover (barricades) and concealment

It should not even be a point of debate that the above aspects be included in a close protection-related competency assessment. However, there are several more aspects that are relevant to close protection. These should include but not be limited to:

+ The ability to prepare relevant personnel, firearms, and equipment required before an operation
+ The ability to apply knowledge and understanding of the tactical operational procedures and techniques (close protection IADs: such as shooting while evacuating a Principal)
+ The ability to conduct post-operational debriefings with relevant personnel.

Based on the above, a relevant close protection shooting assessment should include tests and exercises that not only demonstrate basic handgun competency but also the candidate's ability to utilize the firearm in duty-related situations. Some suggestions of this could be:

+ Demonstration by single operative of drawing and firing while protecting the Principal
+ Demonstration of basic close protection team reactions (performed from formations and walking drills) to simulated attacks (IADs), live fire[25]
+ Demonstration of firing from vehicles during embus/debus or close protection related situations.

It is not recommended that a competency assessment be made so difficult that most candidates would not qualify, nor should it be so easy that a person with average firearm skills could qualify easily. There needs to be an effective middle ground that can actually be applied in practice within the context of the internationally accepted Close Protection industry.

Obviously, a CPO should strive for the highest possible level of firearms competency since this is the maximum force option that if needed, will save lives.

It should be noted that in many countries private security officers such as CPOs are not permitted to carry firearms. Obviously if a CPO was being trained to operate only in such an environment then tactical firearm training would not be relevant. However, a candidate should

---

[25] Live fire means that the drill is performed by firing live ammunition at designated targets. The use of live fire makes the assessment more realistic and lifelike. This enables the assessor to evaluate how the candidate is likely to perform if a real attack took place.

still be able to disarm an armed attacker and have a basic understanding of firearms as he/she may have to defend against them.

Unarmed Combat

This aspect is considered a vital component for well-rounded CPOs who have minimum force options available to them and are able to operate internationally. The details are found earlier on in this book, e.g., "Use of force options" and "close protection" and include the need for CPOs to have competency in unarmed combat, alternative, and improvised weaponry. The feedback obtained from the vast majority of experts indicated that it was important that an assessment covering this topic be focused on outcomes and not orientated towards a candidate's choice of fighting style or system. It was also stated that it is perhaps more important that a candidate is able to deal effectively with work-related situations instead of being able to demonstrate technical competency in specific techniques. This approach is congruent with that of Leroy Thompson who states that:

> *"No one martial art is better for those in*
> *close protection than any other, although one that*
> *incorporates blocks, strikes, throws, arm bars,*
> *kicks, disarming techniques, offense, and defense*
> *with impact weapons and blades and*
> *situational awareness is most desirable."*

Furthermore, it was determined that it is more important that a candidate be able to demonstrate effective attributes under stress, than being able to demonstrate sets of techniques against unrealistic "set up" attacks. Some of the attributes should be:

+ aggression
+ commitment
+ ability to utilize the correct force option under pressure
+ power
+ focus

The above are just examples and the list could obviously be increased and adjusted.

The key concept when analyzing how CPOs could be assessed for this competency could be summarized as follows: The CPO must be able to effectively manage (neutralize, incapacitate, or restrain) an assailant within the constraints of the law in a close protection-related environment (the aim being to protect the Principal) utilizing unarmed combat and/or alternative weaponry to achieve the best result in the most effective manner. It is important that these skills are integrated with IADs and can be performed in a simulated environment, i.e., simulate real-life situations that the candidate may encounter during a CPO operation.

An example of what an assessment should test in candidates could be as follows:

+ Demonstrate ability to strike effectively with different natural body weapons
+ Demonstrate the ability to restrain and control an attacker standing or on the ground
+ Demonstrate the ability to defend against various weapon attacks (close range firearm, knife, baton, etc.)
+ Demonstrate the necessary attributes needed to manage and deal with a violent attack within the constraints of the law while applying effective close protection methodology.

The above is simply a suggested approach based on information obtained from the research. It is suggested that an industry-accepted minimum standard competency assessment be developed and implemented in order to standardize what can be deemed as an "operationally competent" CPO.

Protective Skills

Although almost the same as the subdivision on CPO skills described earlier in this chapter, protective skills can be defined as any physical skill needed to ensure the safety of a Principal other than the use of firearm, alternative weapon, or unarmed combat. This aspect was included to allow experts the opportunity to add any aspects they felt were relevant to protective skills that may not have been previously discussed.

Primarily, experts reiterated the need for a candidate to be competent in the relevant application of formations, embus, debus, walking drills, and related exercises. Since there are no universal textbook right or wrong ways to demonstrate many of these aspects it was mentioned that a generic approach to assessment should be adopted. In other words, the candidate should be assessed on his/her workplace application and choice of protection tactic based on the situation as opposed to demonstrating every option in a repetitive fashion. A written evaluation could also be implemented to assess the CPOs basic understanding of related security concepts.

The primary concept outlined under this topic is for all the relevant subdivisions of a close protection operation to function in a holistic manner. It is vital that all sub-components (see earlier chapter for more information) link synergistically to enable the CPO to provide effective protection for his/her Principal in any situation. This would best be assessed in a scenario-based evaluation where candidates should demonstrate their ability to provide an integrated protective initiative.

The scenario should encompass all the aspects that would be needed to run an effective protection operation,[26] i.e., candidates are provided with a "Principal" (possibly one of the instructors) who has a fictional background and is faced with an imaginary threat. Assessors could be on hand to grade and assess the candidates. The students would also be evaluated on all the necessary documentation (principal profile, threat and risk assessment, operations appreciation, advance work notes, Operations Order, etc.) which they should have prepared during the exercise.

First Aid Skills

The desired level of competency with regard to a CPO's first aid and medical assistance skills can be analyzed from several points of view. Competent international close protection operatives who may have to work in third world countries that do not have sufficient medical facilities and personnel would obviously need a higher first-aid skill level than those operating in developed countries.

The vast majority of CPOs would only be operational where high-quality medical care is available. Therefore, the CPO would only need "immediate responder" first aid training as it would not take too long for more qualified help to arrive or to evacuate the wounded to a medical facility. This view is endorsed by Leroy Thompson who states:

> *"The US Secret Service and many other protective*
> *teams practice what is called 'ten minute medicine',*
> *based on the assumption that the job of the*
> *protective team is to keep the Principal alive*
> *for ten minutes until reaching a*
> *hospital or until emergency medical*
> *technicians can attend."*

Another point raised by several respondents was that in cases where medical concerns were an issue or the Principal was traveling to a country without sufficient medical facilities, a designated qualified medic could be included in the close protection team. This would negate the need for all CPOs to have a very high level of medical training as a designated medic could join the team to fill this gap.

Specialized sessions can be held by registered training providers to deal in more detail with issues such as gun shot wounds and the like. These sessions would be add-on training for experienced CPOs who feel that they may need to operate in an environment in which they will personally have to apply these skills.

---

[26] All aspects of a protection task would involve starting with the planning and advance work and ending with a team debrief. The scenario should ideally run for at least 48 hours.

Security Knowledge

This subject does not concern the subdivisions of protective concepts and CPO skills that have already been discussed in this chapter. The focus of this topic is on related fields of security specialty.

This was discussed in much detail with most of the experts during research for this book and they were of the opinion that a CPO should have a basic understanding of related specialty fields. It was not necessary for the CPO to become an expert in these fields but to simply have a basic understanding (i.e., a working knowledge) of what these fields entail.

The fields that were identified as relevant were: physical security (including alarm systems and access control), risk management, electronic countermeasures (ECM), information technology (IT) security, and investigation. The consensus among the respondents was that while it was important for the CPO to at least know what these specialty fields are about, it is not necessary for any sort of minimum standard competency evaluation to be established.

The reasoning behind this was that if such services are required, it would not be difficult to gain access to the relevant specialist.

In terms of further education, there are several specific courses available on these related topics for CPOs who want to increase their knowledge and qualifications. There are also many opportunities for CPOs to study for security-related tertiary qualifications. Gaining higher level qualifications could expand their employment prospects. This would expose them to more opportunities in the security field other than only close protection, including perhaps the function of a security manager.

Advanced Driver Training

This topic can be grouped under our third essential outcome (protect a Principal during foot, transit, or venue movement). It can be delivered as a stand-alone specialty and generally would have the following aspects in place:

+ protective escort techniques while in transit
+ defensive driving
+ offensive driving
+ evasive driving
+ convoy and motorcade driving

When the methods of assessment were discussed with experts, the feedback was quite ambiguous. The practicality of implementing comprehensive assessment of the above topics would be extremely difficult, especially in private sector training. The reasoning behind this is that the costs of renting/buying vehicles; maintaining and replacing damaged vehicles, skidpans, and race track rentals; and organizing the necessary objects to ram would be exorbitant in comparison with what potential training candidates could afford to pay.

It would perhaps be more practical to make the minimum standard a combination of basic defensive driving with skidpan drills and convoy procedures. Before a candidate performs a practical driving evaluation, a basic theoretical evaluation should be conducted to ensure that the candidate has the necessary theoretical understanding of defensive, offensive, and convoy driving. This should be done in order to ensure the safety of all parties involved since if the candidate does not have a good theoretical base, he/she should not be permitted to perform any practical evaluation.

A suggested example of a close protection driving assessment could cover the following aspects:

+ Pre-trip inspection of the vehicle
+ Observation and awareness of surroundings while driving
+ Vehicle control
+ Application of security concepts (e.g., leaving escape routes, positioning the vehicle in such a way that threats could be minimized, scanning for threats, etc.) while driving
+ Demonstrate knowledge of the Principal positions while in a vehicle
+ Demonstrate understanding of motorcade driving, explaining vehicle positioning, roles, and duties of each vehicle as well as the application of anti-ambush drills (a three-car convoy would be sufficient to demonstrate competency)
+ Be able to demonstrate, on a skidpan or similar surface, the relevant collision avoidance and skid-control techniques
+ Demonstrate the ability to control the vehicle at high speed (this could be built into a further training course if safety is a concern)
+ Be able to demonstrate basic offensive and anti-ambush techniques such as reverse turns and handbrake turns.[27]

The above could form the basis for a close protection driving competency assessment and has been compiled in order to assist training providers in curriculum development as well as for the potential candidate to determine if the training provider of their choice covers the subject in enough detail.

---

[27] Reverse turns and hand-brake turns are evasive maneuvers that would be used if an ambush/roadblock was encountered. These techniques enable the vehicle to quickly turn around and evacuate in the opposite direction of an attack.

It goes without saying that, if possible, a candidate should undergo as extensive training as possible. If not initially in a candidate's basic CPO course, then later in his/her career, a high speed and ramming course should be mandatory.

Protocol and Etiquette

Protocol was consistently mentioned by experts as a point of concern when discussing areas of importance to professional CPO performance. The difficulty seems to become apparent when possible assessment criteria were discussed with the experts. The majority felt that protocol and etiquette was best evaluated during a scenario or similar-type exercise where a candidate would have to demonstrate the necessary attributes (see earlier chapters for more information) in a work-related simulation.

Protocol-related aspects could also be assessed in a theoretical format by using both written or oral questioning to determine candidates' knowledge and understanding, not only of the necessary protocol and etiquette but its practical application.

Management and Business Skills

In terms of a minimum competency assessment for CPOs, the subject of business management skills would not be very important. It may be more relevant when assessing planning officers or team leaders. The business-related skills that would be vital for a CPO to possess would at the very least include:

+ report writing
+ basic budgeting
+ basic computer literacy
+ rudimentary client liaison and marketing skills

Conclusion – Summary of Key Points

In summary, this book has been written to "identify the steps needed to professionalize the Close Protection industry." In-depth interviews, literature review, and the author's personal experience have been used to provide a guide for the reader. The research indicated that ineffective regulation of the Close Protection industry, as well as factors such as content of training, instructor credentials, training methodology, and lack of universal training standards were aspects of concern.

Key fundamentals identified for a country to have effective regulation and standards setting were:

+ A minimum standard covering each accepted area of close protection training to form the basis for a recognized qualification.

♦ A regular re-evaluation and competency assessment framework to maintain up-to-date records of qualified CPOs as well as to clarify their operational status (ability to perform skills in terms of minimum standard requirements).

♦ A penalty system, perhaps a disciplinary system with fines and sanctions that would serve as a deterrent to companies or individuals that do not comply with the above.

♦ A validation database for clients to verify the qualifications of close protection providers.

The concept of an accepted minimum standard that encompasses the identified relevant aspects of Close Protection is a vital component towards professionalizing the close protection industry. This accepted standard must divide the competencies into the relevant subfields and then provide a guideline to measure and quantify exactly what a competent CPO should be able to do.

There are certain key areas that can be identified as vital components of any CPO's skills and knowledge base. These areas refer to some of the hard skills of close protection (i.e., unarmed combat, driving, and firearms) as well as the necessary soft skills (i.e., protocol, report writing, and communication skills). Assessments should evaluate a CPO's knowledge and skills in terms of both theoretical understanding and practical ability. The assessment should attempt to evaluate a CPO's knowledge and skills in terms of what is the minimum accepted standard. If a CPO complies with these minimum standards he/she would be regarded as being competent.

Furthermore, use of scenarios and reality-based simulations should be utilized as evaluation tools wherever possible. This is important, as it is necessary for evaluations to assess what a CPO actually needs to be able to do in order to operate effectively. Eliminating preconceived ideas and focusing on the application of skills should be applied in all aspects of evaluations. These scenarios and assessments should take place in both "live" and controlled environments. The safety of all parties involved in the assessment process should be the first consideration when designing and implementing any practical and scenario assessments.

In conducting research for this book industry experts were interviewed and given the opportunity to outline what they believed were relevant aspects in the establishment of minimum competency standards for the subcategories of close protection. It is important to ensure that standards are not set so high that prospective CPOs cannot qualify. Additionally, standards should not be so low that incompetent persons could qualify as CPOs.

It should also be noted that any assessment and/or minimum standards must, in practical terms, be able to be implemented especially with reference to cost and available resources. The underlying goals of having minimum competency and established assessment criteria are to establish a qualifications framework for CPOs that would be internationally recognized.

It is hoped that the findings and suggestions outlined in this book will be of use to the reader and that many of the suggestions will be implemented in some way to assist in professionalizing the close protection industry worldwide.

As a direct result of globalization, a professional industry with internationally benchmarked qualifications is necessary so that qualified CPOs may gain international recognition for their skills and operate worldwide in this competitive niche market of security services.

Appendix: Definitions

The definitions below have been taken directly from the Dynamic Alternatives (Pty) Ltd. *Basic Close Protection Manual 2003* and in some cases expanded or adapted to fit definitions emanating from the research. Permission has been given in writing for these definitions to be included in this book.

Areas of Responsibility and Arcs of Fire
Refers to the predetermined zones or areas in a close protection formation that are allocated to a team member in advance depending on formation, environment, and the team member's position to other team members and the Principal.

Attack
Any potential, actual, or attempted direct or indirect physical breach and/or threat to the security of the Principal or his/her assets, commercial ventures, as well as any other legal or personal interests and entities, both locally and internationally.

OR

Any potential, actual, or attempted direct or indirect breach and threat to the security and integrity of all restricted information or of any information system relating to the day-to-day functioning of the Principal and/or his/her assets, commercial ventures, or any other legal as well as personal interests or entities, both locally and internationally.

Attempt
A direct or indirect endeavor to breach the security and/or safety of the Principal, his assets, commercial ventures, or restricted information relating to the day-to-day functioning of the Principal.

Client
The client is the organization, body, or person that is actually financing the protection operation. In certain cases the client may also be the Principal, i.e., the person receiving the protection also pays for it.

Clock System
This is a method of communicating between close protection team members. It describes the direction of potential threats based on the numbers of a clock. The direction the Principal is facing is always considered as 12 o'clock.

Close Protection

Those measures taken by a trained individual or team, static or mobile, overt or covert, in order to continuously ensure the safety and comfort of the Principal in a professional manner.

Cover

There are two types of cover:

Cover from sight – any structure or object that will hide something from view

Cover from fire – any structure or object that will prevent projectiles from firearms from penetrating it

Covert Visit

A visit is classified as covert when the visitor and/or the circumstances surrounding the visit is of such a sensitive nature that disclosure could lead to severe damage or serious embarrassment to the Principal, his country, or the country being visited.

Directional Approach

This is a simplified version of the clock systems where the numbers of a clock are substituted with four directions front, back, left, and right. As with the clock system bearing is taken from the direction the Principal is facing.

Divert

This is the action of deflecting or drawing off the attention from one thing or person to another with the aim of getting rid of the hindrance.

Engage/Neutralize

To enter into conflict with any potential threat and render it ineffective by opposite force or effect.

Escorting

This incorporates the physical accompanying of the Principal in a restricted area in order to enhance security. As well as assistance to the Principal with regards to his traveling or visiting program, it also includes all measures, junctions and instructions not relating to safeguarding or protection.

Evacuate

The removal of a person or persons from a place considered to be dangerous, preferably according to a pre-arranged plan.

Immediate Action Drill (IAD)

A planned, trained response to an attack or threatening situation in any given environment.

Liaise

To act as a communication and information link, on behalf of the Principal, with other teams or units and relevant authorities, as well as any external parties involved in a close protection operation.

Overt Visit

A visit is classified as overt when the visitor and the circumstances surrounding the visit are of such a nature that disclosure will not lead to damage or embarrassment to the Principal, his country, or the country being visited.

Principal

A person who as a result of his/her appointment and considering such person's stature/the position he/she fills or the knowledge he/she possesses, is in the national interest that he/she enjoys special handling and protection. The Principal is the person that the protection team actually protects.

Principal Briefing

The briefing given to a new Principal outlining the following: close protection principles and objectives, team modus operandi, the Principals' responsibilities, and any other information deemed relevant for the smooth performance of operations.

Protection

This incorporates continuous close protection, either static or mobile, of the Principal and his/her immediate entourage.

Risk

A condition where loss or losses are possible or a combination of hazards measured against probability/likelihood of the said action/ event actually occurring.

Security Audit

A security audit is a comprehensive evaluation and analysis of all security aspects both physical and other. The security audit is used to determine security weaknesses. Recommendations would then be made on how to minimize the identified weaknesses. A site survey is the physical inspection and assessment of a building or physical structure in order to identify any physical hazards or security risks.

Support

To lend assistance to the Principal, fellow team members, or relevant authorities as a situation demands or requires.

Threat

This refers to any institution, person, organization, item, or condition that has the ability to threaten the physical safety and/or wellbeing of the Principal and/or his/her assets, commercial ventures, or any other legal entity, both locally and internationally.

OR

Any institution, person, organization, item, or condition that has the ability to threaten or damage the public and professional image, dignity, and/or integrity of the Principal and/or his assets, commercial ventures, or any other legal or personal interests or entities, both locally and internationally.

LIST OF REFERENCES

Literary References

Alexander, Y. and Brenner E.H. *Terrorism and the Law*. New York: Transnational Publishers, 2001.

Behaviour Systems Development (Pty) Ltd. *Train the Trainer Manual*. Pretoria: Behaviour Systems Development (Pty) Ltd., 2003 (a).

Behaviour Systems Development (Pty) Ltd. *Skills Assessor Course Manual*. Pretoria: Behaviour Systems Development (Pty) Ltd., 2003 (b).

Braunig, M. *The Executive Protection Bible*. Aspen: ESI Education Development Organisation, 1993.

British and Foreign Bible Society. *The Holy Scriptures of the Old Testament*. London: The British and Foreign Bible Society, 1965.

Bruyns, H., Kriel, J., Minnaar, A., Mistry, D., Pillay, K., and Snyman, R. *Guidelines for Research Proposal Writing. Masters, and Doctoral Students*. Florida: Technikon SA Faculty of Public Safety and Criminal Justice, 2001.

Calibre Press. *Surviving Edged Weapons*. Northbrook: Calibre Press Video Production, 1987.

Consterdine. P. *Streetwise: The Complete Manual of Personal Security and Self Defence*. Leeds: Summersdale Press, 1997.

Consterdine, P. *The Modern Bodyguard: The Manual of Close Protection Training*. Leeds: Protection Publications, 1995.

Cunningham, W.C. and Taylor, T.H. *Crime and Protection in America: A Study of Law Enforcement Resources and Relationships*. Mclean: Hallcrest Systems Inc., 1985.

Davies, B. *Terrorism: Inside a World Phenomenon*. London: Virgin Books Ltd., 2003.

Dynamic Alternatives (Pty) Ltd. *Basic Close Protection Instructional Manual.* Pretoria: Dynamic Alternatives (Pty) Ltd., 2002.

Elhanan. P. *Keep 'em Alive: The Bodyguard's Trade.* Boulder: Paladin Press, 1985.

Gloria, D. *UBUNTU Training Academy. Security Officers Self Study Manuals: Grades A to E, 2004.* Arcadia : UBUNTU Training Academy.

Government Gazette. *Anti-terrorism Bill.* Gazette number 24076, 15 November 2002. Pretoria: Government Printers, 2002.

Government Gazette. *Judicial Matters Amendment Bill.* Gazette number 27001, 18 November 2004: Government Printers, 2004.

Haney. E.L. *Inside Delta Force.* London: Corgi Books, 2002.

Hoffman, B. 1998. *Inside Terrorism.* London: Victor Gollancz

Jacobs, L. & Schneider, G. *Report and Recommendations after Training and Operations with the Presidential Protection Unit of Equatorial Guinea.* Malabo: unpublished internal report for Securicor Gray (Pty) Ltd., 2002.

Jorgensen, D.L. *Participant Observation: A Methodology for Human Studies.* Newbury Park: Sage, 1990.

King, J.A. *Providing Protective Services.* Shawnee mission: Varro Press. 2001.

Laqueur, W. *The New Terrorism.* London: Phoenix Press, 1999.

Locke L.F., Silverman, S.J. & Spirduso, W. 1998. *Reading and Understanding Research.* Thousand Oaks: Sage

Minnaar, A. *Inaugural Lecture. Private-Public Partnerships: Private Security, Crime Prevention and Policing in South Africa.* Florida: Department of Security Risk Management, School of Criminal Justice, College of Law, UNISA, 2004.

Mistry, D., Minnaar, A., Redpath J. & Dhlamini, J. *Research Report: Use of Force by Members of the South African Police Services: Case Studies from Seven Policing Areas in Gauteng.* Florida Institute for Human rights and Criminal Justice research, Technikon South Africa, 2001.

Mouton, J. *How to Succeed in Your Masters and Doctoral Studies.* Pretoria: Van Schaik, 2001.

Musselman, V.A. & Jackson, J.H. *Introduction to Modern Business. Ninth Edition.* New Jersey: Prentice-Hall, Inc., 1984.

Nicholls-Steyn & Associates (Pty) Ltd. *Basic VIP Protection Instructional Manual*. Johannesburg: Nicholls-Steyn & Associates (Pty) Ltd., 1999.

Oatman, R.L. *The Art of Executive Protection*. Baltimore: Noble House, 1999.

Rapp, B. and Lesce, T. *Bodyguarding: A Complete Manual*. Washington: Loompanics Unlimited, 1995.

South African Qualifications Authority. *Unit Standard 10748: Use of a Handgun*. Pretoria: South African Qualifications Authority.

South African Qualifications Authority. *Unit Standard 10757: Use of Firearms in Tactical Duty Related Situations*. Pretoria: South African Qualifications Authority.

South African Qualifications Authority. *Unit Standard 11510: Provide Close Protection of Designated Persons*. Pretoria: South African Qualifications Authority.

Schönteich, M. "South Africa's Arsenal of Terrorism Legislation." *African Security Review*, 9(2): 39–51. 2000. (http://www.iss.org.za/Pubs/ASR/9No2/Schonteich.html. Accessed 16 November 2004)

Shackley, T.G., Oatman, R.L. and Finney, R.A. *You're the Target: Coping with Terror and Crime*. Virginia: New World Publishing. 1989.

Steyn, R. *One Step Behind Mandela*. Johannesburg: Zebra Press. 2000.

Technikon SA. *Code of Ethics for Research at Technikon SA*. Section 7. December 2000. Florida: TSA, 2000.

Thompson, G. *Dead or Alive*. London: Summersdale Press, 1999.

Thompson, L. *The Bodyguard Manual: Protection Techniques of the Professionals*. London: Greenhill Books, 2003.

Section 22 of the United States codes (http://www.access.gpo.gov/uscode/title22/chapter26_.html. Accessed 16 July 2004)

Wordsworth Reference. *Sun Tzu: The Art of War*. Hertfordshire: Wordsworth Reference, 1993.

Welman, J.C. Kruger, S.J. *Research Methodology for the Business and Administrative Sciences*. South Africa: Thomson Publishing Company, 1999.

Internet

(Websites accessed for background information)

African Digital Library. 17 Jan. 2004 <http://www.netlibrary.com>. (background on close protection in Africa)

Australian National Training Information Service. December 2003–March 2004 <http://www.ntis.gov.au>. (background information on close protection training and standards in Australia)

Australian Professional Bodyguards. 10 December 2003 <http://www.apbodyguards.com.au>. (background on close protection in Australia)

Criminal Justice Resources for Security Management. 16 November 2004 <http://www.lib.msu.edu/harris23/crimjust/secman.htm> (background on regulation of private security in the USA)

Dynamic Alternatives (Pty) Ltd. July–November 2004 <http://www.dynamicaltenatives.co.za>. (background on close protection services and training)

General information on South Africa (11-04) U.S. Department of State. November–December 2004 <http://www.state.gov/r/pa/ei/bgn/2898.htm>.

Institute for Security Studies. September–November 2004 <http://www.iss.co.za>. (background information on terrorism in South Africa)

International Bodyguard Association. December 2004–January 2005 <http://www.unique.fu8.com/ibabodyguards/main.php>. (background information on Close Protection)

Knowledge UK. 10 March 2004 <http://www.britishcouncil.org>. (background on close protection in the UK)

Links to Australian Industry Training Accreditation Boards (ITABs) and Recognised Bodies. December 2003–March 2004 <http://www.anta.gov.au/lnkItabs.asp>. (background information on close protection in Australia)

London City and Guilds. January–March 2004 <http://www.city-and-guilds.co.uk>. (background on close protection training in the UK)

Nicholls-Steyn and Associates. 20 March 2004 <http://www.nicholls-steyn.com>. (background on close protection services and training)

NSW Police Online Security Industry Registry. December 2003–March 2004 <http://www.police.nsw.gov.au/security_industry_registry>. (background information on close protection and private security regulation in Australia)

Professional Bodyguard Association. December 2004–January 2005 <http://www.bodyguards-pba.com>. (background information on Close Protection)

South African government info. September 2004–March 2005 <http://www.info.gov.za/documents/combsubst.htm>. (background on legislation applicable to private security and close protection)

Statistical info. 20 March 2004 <http://www.statssa.go.za>. (crime statistics)

Task International. 20 March 2004 <http://www.taskinternational.com>. (background on close protection services and training)

Technikon Pretoria. 20 June–1 July 2003 <http://www.techpta.ac.za>.

The Australian Institute for Criminology. December 2003–February 2004 <http://www.aic.gov.au>. (background on close protection in Australia)

The POSLEC SETA Home Page. March–November 2004 <http://www.poslecseta.org.za>. (information on POSLEC SETA)

The Private Security Industry Regulatory Authority. March–November 2004 <http://www.sira-sa.co.za>. (background on PSIRA)

The South African Police Services. July–November 2004 <http://www.saps.org.za>. (crime statistics)

The UK home office. February–November 2004 <http://www.homeoffice.gov.uk>. (background on private security industry regulation)

U.S Department of State. 24 November 2004 <http://www.state.gov/www/global/terrorism/1998Report/appb.html>. (background on international terror groups)

U.S State Department travel advisory for South Africa. November 2004 <http://travel.state.gov/travel/safrica.html>. (travel advice for visitors to South Africa)

United States Code – Electronic Edition. November–December 2004 <http://www.access.gpo.gov/uscode>.

United States, Overseas Security Advisory Council. November–December 2004 <http://www.ds-osac.org/sitemap.cfm>. (background on international terrorist threats)

Vocational Educational and Training Accreditation Board (VETAB) Australia. March–April 2004 <http://www.vetab.nsw.gov.au>. (background information on close protection training and standards in Australia)

Interviews

The descriptions below were current at the time of interview the author takes no responsibility for any changes to status or details that may have occurred sine the time of interview.

Interview 1: David Sharp. Pretoria. 1 May 2003. International Verifier for Task International on Close Protection training and standards. British assessor, moderator and verifier for National Vocational Qualifications in the UK.

Interview 2: Lourens Jacobs. Pretoria. 5 May 2003. Former Commander Presidential Protection Unit, SAPS; specialized consultant, instructor and team leader for close protection-related tasks.

Interview 3: Johan Van Eck. Durban. 11 May 2003. Former operative VIP Protection Unit and close protection instructor specialized training services, SAPS; Manager of Executive Protection Standard Bank South Africa based in Johannesburg.

Interview 4: Clinton McGuire. Durban. 12 May 2003. Former close protection operative, SANDF, Freelance close protection specialist; Director of Dynamic Alternatives (Pty) Ltd a specialist close protection training company based in Pretoria.

Interview 5: Jarred Higgins. Johannesburg. 2 June 2003. Close protection specialist, General Manager Nicholls-Steyn and Associates, which at the time of the interiew was the largest close protection company in South Africa.

Interview 6: Norman Steynberg. Johannesburg. 7 June 2003. Former close protection instructor, SANDF; Chief Instructor High Risk Close Protection for Special Forces, SANDF.

Interview 7: Stephan Hugo. Centurion. 15 June 2003. Former Commander VIP Protection training, SAPS and Executive Protection Manager for BMW, South Africa.

Interview 8: Gordon Sekwati Thobejane. Pretoria. 10 July 2003. Close protection specialist, SAAF; Sergeant Major operating as a Supervisor of close protection training in the SAAF based in Pretoria.

Interview 9: Wayne Hendricks. Johannesburg. 16 July 2003. Close protection specialist; Former member of the Presidential Protection Unit, SAPS and personal bodyguard to Nelson Mandela; Head of Executive Protection at Goldman Sachs, South Africa.

Interview 10: Russell Jones. Johannesburg. 30 July 2003. Close protection specialist and registered close protection Assessor with the POSLEC SETA.

Interview 11: Hennie Richards. Midrand. 19 August 2003. CEO of the Police, Private Security, Legal, Correctional Services & Justice Sector Education & Training Authority (POSLEC SETA).

Interview 12: Rory Steyn. Johannesburg. 14 October 2003. Close protection specialist and former Presidential Protection Unit, SAPS; personal bodyguard to Nelson Mandela; Owner/Director of Nicholls-Steyn and Associates.

Interview 13: Gal Allon. Tel Aviv, Israel. A series of informal interviews took place during September 2003. Vice director and instructor of Global Hit Security, a close protection deployment and training company in Israel.

Interview 14: John Garvey. Sydney, Australia. A series of informal interviews took place during January 2004. Director of Corporate Protection Services Pty (Ltd), specialist security consulting and training company in Australia.

Interview 15: Timothy Irvine-Smith, Cape Town. 23 April 2004. Director of RONIN, a specialist close protection training company based in Cape Town.

Interview 16: Neil Maharaj. Pretoria. 8 May 2004. Former police CPO and trainer, involved in industry Standard Generating Body (SGB) and training material developer.

Interview 17: Morne Van Rooyen. Pretoria. 8 May 2004. Major in the SAAF, close protection specialist and coordinator of the SAAF Close Protection Unit based in Pretoria.

Interview 18: Chris Rootman. Johannesburg. 10 July 2004. Secretary VIP Protectors Association of South Africa (VIPPASA). Owner of the close protection company, Protectour, based in Hartebeespoort.

Interview 19: Ash Bodhoo. Pretoria. 18 August 2004. Head of Law Enforcement and Training at the Private Security Industry Regulatory Authority (PSIRA).

Interview 20: D.J. Van Jaarsveld. Pretoria. 6 November 2004. Senior Superintendent in SAPS, Sub-section: Head of Development Services.

Endorsements for *Beyond the Bodyguard*:

"I have personally known Gavriel Schneider for the last 12 years. He is a straight, upright, honorable, and respected man in the capacity of body-guarding and self-defense. He has a high grade in Dennis Survival Ju-Jitsu and many other styles, with many years experience in teaching and training.

His book on bodyguarding is straight to the point and is of high quality. I use it personally in the Dennis Survival Ju-Jitsu system."

—Dr. Dennis Hanover – Kaicho Dennis Hanover is a 10th Dan Grand-master. He is Life President of Dennis Survival Ju-jitsu as well as Life President of the Original European Jujitsu Union (EJJU).

"I have had the pleasure of reading your in-depth research, 'An Examination of the Required Operational Skills and Training Standards for a Close Protection Operative.' As this book is based on the research, I can say that from experience I can recommend this to all who are involved in the executive protection field. In addition to being well written and thoroughly researched, it is comprehensive and detailed. It is my wish that this book be used as a reference for all executive protection operations and training; we can all learn and better ourselves."

—Eytan Nevo – Nevo is a former officer in the Israel defence Force (IDF); his last post was as the head of a special hostage rescue/negotiation team at the counter ter- ror unit. He is a recognized specialist in aviation security and National Key Point Protection with an extensive history of coordination and training of close protection officers, including CPO's for leading political parties and other organizations.

"I would like to commend Gavriel Schneider on his comprehensive research and would recommend this book to any person serious about security. I have had extensive experience in the fields of Close Protection and counter-terror- ism but have still found this work to be very beneficial. As an international verifier I had the pleasure of verifying Gavriel Schneider against the British standards several years ago. I have found him to be well versed not only in the theoretical aspects of close protection but in the practical aspects required for operational deployment."

—Major David M. Sharp (ret) – Sharp was a former Major in the British Military where the majority of his time was spent in Special Forces. David is considered an in- ternational expert on close protection and specialist security and serves as a high-level consultant to many global organizations and several governments as well as a verifier for City and Guilds, one of the United Kingdoms' premier certification bodies.

"I have known Gavriel Schneider for over a decade, During this time we have not only become great friends and colleagues but he has proved himself as a skilled close protection operator and trainer and has always maintained a high level of professionalism. His efforts and contributions to make the CPO industry respected and understood are well noted. We have trained presidential, African royal family and Special Forces protection operators as well as deployed operationally in high-risk environments including protection of presidents, celebrities and senior-level business executives. This experience and his thorough research have combined to make this book on Close Protection a must read for anyone involved in the protection environment."

—*Clinton McGuire – McGuire is the Managing Director of Dynamic Alternatives, which is a specialized security consultancy and training organization. He has had over 15 years of close protection experience at all levels. Prior to entering the private sector Clinton was a member of a South African Defense Force (SADF) specialist military unit. He has also served as a member of the close protection task team responsible for formulating the close protection training standards in South Africa.*

"Gavriel Schneider has been a friend and colleague to me for the past seven years. It has been my pleasure to be associated with him both on a personal and business level. Although he is highly trained and qualified in several styles of martial arts, he is a humble and self-disciplined individual. He is also a great businessman and one which I have learned all that I know about business. He is also a great motivator and one that leads by example.

Gavriel was the first recipient of a master's degree in security studies in South Africa. His thesis was "Professionalizing the Close Protection Industry in South Africa." The paper was thoroughly researched and has become the handbook of reference for close protection professionals in the country. A lot of the subject matter has been incorporated into the qualifications standard of the Close Protection industry."

— *Chris Hazis – Hazis was a Lt-Colonel in the South African Police Services. He left the service after 18 years. Chris was the Provincial Commander of the VIP Protection Unit as well as the co-ordinator of Presidential protection for the region. He is now involved in close protection within the private sector*

Lightning Source UK Ltd.
Milton Keynes UK
UKOW030039170112

185473UK00002B/96/P